Advance praise for
The Ivey Guide to Law School Admissions

"*The Ivey Guide to Law School Admissions* is the book I wish I'd had when applying to law school. The *Ivey Guide* is quite simply the first and best resource for law school applicants." —Marshall Camp, JD2B.com

"Admissions officers around the country will be wringing their hands over this book—it will be difficult to reject applicants who follow Ms. Ivey's timely, witty, and practical tips." —Lyle Roberts, partner at Wilson Sonsini Goodrich & Rosati

"Finally, a law school guide that tells it like it is! From how law schools break down their applicant pool to what really sets an applicant apart, there is no more intimate or current an account of the law school admissions process than the *Ivey Guide*." —Gail P. Dave, Vice President and Counsel, Deutsche Bank AG

"Law school applicants everywhere will find Anna Ivey's book a useful, indeed essential, roadmap for the journey ahead." —James Ho, Law Clerk, U.S. Supreme Court

"Ivey's book is stuffed with the best advice I have ever read for aspiring lawyers. It spells out in concrete detail exactly what it takes to separate yourself from the crowd." —Ross Davies, Former Editor in Chief, *The University of Chicago Law Review*

What students are saying about Anna Ivey

"Anna Ivey guided me through many pitfalls; she offered fantastic and substantive advice along the way. Some pieces of advice were macroscopic, like essay topics; others were as minute as specific words in my résumé. By December, I was in at Stanford. By mid-February, I was in at Yale and Harvard."
—Yale law student

"The only negative about working with Anna Ivey is that every time it's freezing cold here, I have to wonder whether I should have gone to Stanford. She helped put me in the God-awful position of having to choose between the two."
—Harvard law student

"Anna Ivey just has an eye for detail and encouraged me to shed light on things I'd have cast aside as unimportant. How would I know what a law school might find important? I ended up being accepted to my first choice, Michigan, and received a nice grant as well."
—Michigan law student

"With Anna Ivey's help, I went from applications swathed in mediocrity to having to choose among top-ten law schools. I can't recommend her more strongly, and in fact have recommended her to friends and even my own wife."
—University of Pennsylvania law student

The
IVEY GUIDE
to
LAW SCHOOL
ADMISSIONS

The IVEY GUIDE *to* LAW SCHOOL ADMISSIONS

Straight Advice on Essays, Résumés, Interviews, and More

Anna Ivey

Former Dean of Admissions,
The University of Chicago Law School

A Harvest Original
Harcourt, Inc.
Orlando   Austin   New York
San Diego   Toronto   London

www.HarcourtBooks.com

Library of Congress Cataloging-in-Publication Data
Ivey, Anna, 1972–
The Ivey guide to law school admissions: straight advice on essays, résumés, interviews, and more/Anna Ivey.
p. cm.
"A Harvest Original."
1. Law schools—United States—Admission. I. Title: Guide to law school admissions. II. Title.
KF285.I94 2005
340'.071'173—dc22   2004021327
ISBN 0-15-602979-0

Text set in Trump Mediaeval
Designed by G. B. D. Smith

Printed in the United States of America

First edition
K J I H G F E D C B

Acknowledgments

any thanks to the talented and hardworking admissions officers I've worked with and befriended over the years—especially Dick Badger, who was kind enough to admit me to an incomparable law school and university, and to whom I still owe several pizzas for the bets I have lost. Quite a few of you have shared your thoughts on an anonymous basis, and I appreciate your insights even though I can't thank you here by name.

And thank you to the wonderful applicants who have crossed paths with me, and to those who were kind enough to discuss their experiences and share their application materials for this book. I haven't used your names, but you know who you are.

AUTHOR'S NOTE

The examples and sample materials in this book are based on my real-life experiences, but I have concealed applicants' identities throughout, and some of the sample materials are entirely made up. More important: Plagiarism can end your legal career before it even starts, so do not copy any of the content for your applications.

Contents

CHAPTER 1

Straight Answers: Getting Inside the Head of an Admissions Officer

A ll law school admissions officers face a dilemma. There are certain things they *wish* they could tell applicants because it would make their own lives so much easier, but they can't say, "In all honesty, we only spend about five minutes on each file, so you'd better cut to the chase," or, "Please, for the love of god, don't make me read another essay about endangered guppies." And they certainly can't say, "Don't bother applying with a 160 LSAT... unless you're a minority and then we'll throw in a scholarship."

No one will risk getting fired or sued over that, not to mention the PR disaster that would ensue. So they grumble to themselves, prop open their eyelids with matchsticks, and keep reading thousands upon thousands of essays about endangered guppies, year in and year out. How do I know this? Because that was my daily life when I was dean of admissions at the University of Chicago Law School. I denied so many applicants while thinking, "If only they knew!"

Picture this, a typical day for me as an admissions officer (and for just about every other admissions officer): I'm surrounded by hundreds of files stacked on every flat surface in my office. I have, on average, five minutes to read each one and make a decision on its fate. I've already worked my way through more than a thousand files this month, and I've read more than thirty today. I crack open the next one on top of the pile, a file belonging to a woman named Sarah. I scan her application form, her LSAT scores, and her college transcript in less than a minute and conclude that her GPA is just below our GPA median, and that her LSAT score is just above our LSAT median. As dean of admissions, I could easily write an "A" for accept or a "D" for deny at the top of Sarah's file based on this hard data alone, so the fate of her application depends entirely on the remaining four minutes I spend scanning the "soft stuff" of her application: her essay, her recommendations, her résumé, and her addendum. Four minutes, maybe less. That's it.

Most applicants go horribly wrong here—not because the soft stuff of their files suggests that they can't handle law school or reveals them to be arrogant jerks (although that happens, too, from time to time). They go wrong because they have failed to persuade me that I should choose them over thousands of other applicants with acceptable numbers who I know could succeed at my law school. Sarah fails because she didn't wow me, and I'm sure she had no idea how to wow me.

This book shows you how to wow an admissions officer. I've written this book to say all the things that I could never say when I was an admissions officer, even though I really wanted to. But I've also written this book because it's the kind of book I wish I'd had when I was applying to law school.

I've been in your shoes. I remember how heady it felt to decide that I was going to apply to law school. With visions of *Law & Order* dancing in my head, I wanted to shoot for the top, for that all-purpose degree that would offer me the greatest career flexibility and the best financial safety net. I remember how mind-numbingly boring it was to complete those practice LSAT tests day in and day out for months at a time, until I couldn't even go out to dinner with friends without pondering who was going to sit in Seat #2 if Sam won't sit next to a redhead and Julie has to sit across from one of two vegetarians and Seat #4 has to remain empty. I remember that queasy, sleepless night before my LSAT, when I inspected the alarm clock every ten minutes while the hours slipped away. How paralyzed I felt by the range of topics when I sat down to tap out my life story in a two-page essay "on the subject of my choice" that would help the admissions committee "get to know me better." The anxiety of waiting for a response, wondering what was holding things up as I compared notes with other applicants. Law school invaded every single thought that passed through my head for a good nine months, and, despite my rational judgment, a more primordial part of me took over and let the law school admissions process consume my life.

I remember well how daunting the application process was, especially the essays. Did they want me to write about law? I didn't know any yet! Did they want me to prove that I was a genius at logic and rhetoric? Was I supposed to entertain them with my wit and charm? Did they want me to prove that I was applying out of pure motives—for the public good!—and that I wasn't some moneygrubbing status hound? How was I supposed to know any of this, when I didn't even know what kind of people would be reading my file, or how they went about selecting their students? The process was a mystery to me.

The essays were difficult, but at least I had some control over them. Faculty recommendations, on the other hand, felt completely beyond my control. I had no idea at the time what my professors really thought of me, or if some of them would even recognize me if they passed me on the street. I hadn't actively cultivated any relationships for recommendation purposes, because I hadn't appreciated until I sat down with my applications how important those relationships would be, and by then I was certain there wouldn't be enough time for meaningful schmoozing. I also didn't know the appropriate protocol or the etiquette. I didn't know whether it was kosher to draft the letters myself, as some recommenders had requested, and I didn't know how to deal with the professor who kept saying he'd get around to the letter as months went by and deadlines loomed.

The numbers were the biggest mystery to me. Were admissions officers being honest when they insisted that it wasn't just a numbers game? Did my numbers make me a shoo-in? A shoo-out? Were there some schools I shouldn't even be bothering with? How reliable were those LSAT and GPA grids? Would it be a waste of time to continue with my extracurriculars if they were going to bring down my GPA? Should I be loading up on gut classes, or demonstrating my intellectual grit by taking harder classes with lower grade prospects? What classes and activities meant something, and which ones were considered fluff?

It's amazing that I was so clueless, considering the fact that I had applied to and been admitted to plenty of fancy-pants schools by the time I sat down to apply to law school. I took my first standardized admissions test in sixth grade, in order to attend junior high at Boston Latin School; for high school, I attended Phillips Academy Andover, moved on to Columbia College, and spent my junior year at Cambridge University in the UK. Despite all that, the admissions process remained a black box, and off I went to the University of Chicago Law School without any clue as to why these schools had chosen me over my many friends and acquaintances who seemed to have just as much, if not more, to offer. For all I knew, admissions officers just threw darts at a board, and my luck had just been fantastically good. What I didn't know then is that even smart and accomplished people can make stupid (and common) mistakes on their applications. I was lucky in the sense that I avoided some traps without knowing in advance what they were. You shouldn't rely on luck. If you're reading this book, you're already miles ahead of where I was.

Of course, some things have changed for applicants since I applied to law school back in the early 1990s. When we waited for our LSAT scores and our admissions decisions, we ran home every day to check our mailboxes—the bricks-and-mortar kind, not our e-mail in-boxes—several times a day. Good exercise, that. But the biggest difference has to be the way the Internet has changed the application experience. When I was applying, there were no discussion boards where applicants trade admissions war stories and statistics, share intelligence, critique each other's strategies, waste time ("My List of the Ten Sexiest Ugly Women on TV!"), and disseminate more rumors and misinformation than Dan Rather on election night. It's way too much for any one person to process, and it's hard to gauge what information is reliable. Applicants may feel empowered by all the opinions and statements of fact floating around out there, but applicants are just as neurotic and misinformed now as when I was applying; some would say more so.

What hasn't changed is the black-box aspect of law school admissions. Law school admissions officers can't and don't speak candidly about affirmative action, for example, or what kinds of essays make them want to shoot themselves in the head from boredom. (And I don't blame them for that in either case. I've been there.) Law school students, while helpful resources in other ways, generally know nothing about law school admissions except that they got in. And applicants are even less informed, no matter how easy it is these days to find them and compare notes.

I wrote this book to offer applicants straightforward, practical tips from an insider's perspective. I've read thousands of files, conducted hundreds of admissions interviews, and traveled across the country to meet with and counsel hundreds of thousands of prospective applicants at law school forums and pre-law society fairs. More than that, I made the tough choices, the *final* choices, about who got in and who didn't. *The Ivey Guide to Law School Admissions* offers you the benefit of that experience. It tells you the truth without sugarcoating, without the law school PR. My admissions counseling clients have the benefit of my one-on-one advice; this book is the next best alternative.

In *The Ivey Guide to Law School Admissions*, applicants will find answers to questions like these:

- I have an LSAT score of 164. Will that get me into Columbia, my dream school? Is it even worth paying the $70 to apply?

- What kinds of essays do they like? Do they want to hear about my work fighting poverty? My backpacking trip through Europe? My parents' divorce? My marathon training? My analysis of *The Simpsons* as a reflection of the American zeitgeist?

▪ How do race and sex really affect my admissions chances?

▪ Should I write a letter explaining my unrepresentative LSAT score, my D in Organic Chemistry, my attention deficit disorder, my stint in rehab? Or will that make me sound whiny?

▪ Should I submit my poetry, my photography portfolio, my master's thesis, my karaoke tape?

▪ Am I at a disadvantage as a forty-year-old stay-at-home mom who's applying to law school now that my kids are off to college? Will law schools take me seriously?

▪ Can I use the same résumé that I use for job purposes?

▪ For my recommendation, should I necessarily pick the English professor who says she'll write me "a great letter"?

▪ Do I look bad if I cancel my LSAT score and retake it?

Filled with easy-to-follow dos and don'ts, this book shows you how to produce the very best law school applications. You'll find that the advice in this book is geared toward normal people—people who haven't necessarily founded and sold their technology start-ups to Fortune 500 companies for billions of dollars, played pro football, emigrated to this country after surviving the pillaging of their sub-Saharan villages, grown up the children of radical fugitives, or served as test-case plaintiffs in the most pressing constitutional cases of our time. Those folks don't need much help making their applications stand out from the pack or finding dramatic and thrilling essay topics. (But beware: Those people do apply to law school, and they are among your competitors.) Instead, I wrote this book for the vast majority of applicants, the mere mortals who have distinguished themselves on a less dramatic scale and want practical advice on how to present their accomplishments and goals in the best possible and most interesting light.

Ideally you'll start reading this book early in your college career, because some of the strategies I suggest for improving your prospects as an applicant can't be executed overnight. However, there's also more than plenty here for people who are cracking open this book just as they sit down to start work on their applications and need quick answers, as well as for older applicants who are considering a career change and want to get a bird's-eye view of the application process before deciding whether to invest their evenings and weekends in that pursuit.

I also hope that parents of prospective law school applicants read this book. Some parents do their children a real disservice by failing to educate themselves about the current state of the legal profession and the things admissions officers really care about when they're putting together an incoming class. If you have strong opinions about the benefits of a law degree, for example, or of the necessity for going to law school straight out of college, read on ... and please keep an open mind. I know you want what's best for your son or daughter, but ask yourself what you really know about law school, or the legal profession, or the law school admissions process *today*—not twenty or thirty or forty years ago—before you exert your influence one way or another.

I hope this book helps demystify the law school admissions process. If you have suggestions for future editions, please send your comments to comments@iveyguide.com.

CHAPTER 2

The Wow Factor: What Admissions Officers Really Look For

So what exactly do admissions officers do in those five minutes they spend scrutinizing your file, and what distinguishes the files that end up in one pile from those that land in the other?

Admissions officers receive many more applications than they have seats to fill, and each year they turn away enough perfectly qualified people to fill those seats many times over. And admissions officers *know* that those people are perfectly qualified, that they could handle the work and thrive at their law schools. So admissions is really about choosing a handful from among a large number of capable and tempting applicants. Admissions officers are basically in the business of *risk analysis*, which is a fancy way of saying that they have to make quick decisions with limited information.

In this way, admissions officers are not unlike Hollywood producers and their financial backers when they are deciding whether to make a particular movie (that was my bailiwick as a film finance attorney). These people are bombarded with hundreds of scripts every year, but they can't possibly scrutinize every single one. If life were fair, each of these scripts would receive the benefit of a thorough analysis, complete with multiple readings and real thought given to the merits of subject matter, theme, and use of dialogue, but in the real world no one has that much time to spend on these decisions, even though there are often hundreds of millions of dollars at stake.

Instead, producers do what every person does when performing risk analysis: They use shortcuts. Has a big-name director already read the script and liked it? Is a big star championing the script? Does the screenwriter have a proven track record? Or perhaps it's a certain kind of genre that always does well overseas even if the movie doesn't do so well domestically? The person making that decision would prefer to see more than one of these positive indicators—the more indicators, the more likely it is that the movie is going to get made.

For law school admissions officers, great LSAT and GPA numbers are the quickest and easiest indicators—it's like having Steven Spielberg and Tom Cruise signed on to a project, in which case you don't need to worry as much about scrutinizing the script. But obviously plenty of movies get made without Steven Spielberg or Tom Cruise, just as the top schools accept plenty of people without perfect numbers.

THE NUMBERS GAME

The best quick-and-dirty predictor of your competitiveness as an applicant to a particular school is to see how you stack up against what admissions officers call the medians: the median LSAT score and the median GPA of the incoming class admitted the previous year. For example, at Georgetown, the incoming class of 2003 had a median LSAT score of 169, and a median GPA of 3.64. (If you're not sure what a median is, it means that half of the incoming class had LSAT scores below 169, and the other half had scores above 169.)

You can usually find that data for a given school on the admissions page of its website, either in the Frequently Asked Questions (FAQ) section or in the Class Profile section. You can also find data on the 25th and 75th percentile LSAT scores and GPAs in the *ABA-LSAC Official Guide to ABA-Approved Law Schools*, on view for free at www.lsac.org. You won't find the median numbers (that would be the 50th percentile), but you can get a ballpark sense of the upper range you want to fall into. Make sure that you find out the relevant numbers for the most recent incoming class, because a lot can change in just a few years. For example, when applications spike (as they did in 2002 and 2003), schools all up and down the food chain usually are able to ratchet up their LSAT medians by a point or two (say, from 169 to 170) or their GPA medians by a few tenths of a point (say, from 3.65 to 3.75).

Think of your LSAT and GPA as creating *presumptions* in favor of, or against, admitting you. The higher your numbers are for any given school, the less impressive the rest of your application has to be, and the greater the presumption is that you should be admitted. In that case, the admissions officer looks to the rest of your file to see if there's a reason *not* to admit you (more on the most common problems can be found at the bottom of the next page and in Chapter 6). On the flip side, the lower your numbers fall below the medians, the greater the presumption is that you should be denied, and the admissions officer looks to the rest of your file to find out if there are compelling reasons there to overlook the numbers and admit you (maybe because you submitted exceptional essays or recommendations, demonstrated unusual life or work experience, or wowed her in an interview). So your numbers basically determine the *approach* an admissions officer is going to take to the rest of your file: She may be looking for reasons to keep you out (in the case of high numbers), or she may be looking for reasons to let you in (in the case of low numbers).

In practice, about 15 percent of files have numbers so low that they warrant only a quick glance to make sure the admissions officer is not accidentally denying a Pulitzer Prize winner. About another 15 percent of files have numbers so high that the files warrant only a quick glance to make sure the admissions officer is not admitting a convicted embezzler. The other 70 percent that fall in the middle of the curve take up most of her time. That's where she scrutinizes the transcript, the résumé, the essay, and any other parts of the file. What does that mean for you?

▓ If your numbers are very high for a school, your job as an applicant is *not to screw up.*

▓ If your numbers are very low for a school, your job is *to be exceptional.*

▓ If you're in that 70 percent category for a school, your job is *to distinguish yourself from the pack.*

There is some variation from school to school, but the approaches tend to be more alike than they are different. For example, some law schools send all or some of the applications they receive to their professors for review, but those professors have to adhere to the same goals, and be mindful of the same trade-offs, that their admissions officers face. However, there is one difference that you should know about: Public schools tend to be more numbers driven than private schools (which are also quite numbers driven, so we're only talking about a difference in degree), although the top public schools, like Michigan and Berkeley and Texas, function more like private schools in the great attention they pay to the nonnumerical pieces of your application.

If Your Numbers Are Very High

These are some common reasons why people with very high numbers are rejected:

■ Your application reveals that you're an arrogant show-off. Every class at every school on the face of the earth has that one person who is universally reviled by students and faculty alike, and if you're admitted, you're likely to be that person.

■ You have a demonstrated disposition to do or say things that are likely to get you kicked out of law school or the bar, whether it's murder, sexual harassment, fraud, embezzlement, or a taste for heroin.

■ You're an aging, bitter PhD candidate who has never held a real job in her life, is fleeing to law school because she can't find a job on the brutal academic market, doesn't know the first thing about law school, the practice of law, or her post-JD job prospects, and thinks she deserves to be in law school because she's the second coming of Akhil Amar, the legendary Yale Law School professor.

■ You signal a blasé attitude that makes clear you are applying there only as a safety and are unlikely to accept an offer.

If Your Numbers Are Very Low

If your numbers are very low, you really need to be one of those people I referred to in the last chapter—the concert pianist, the pro football player, the gal who has a math theorem named after her, or the kid who grew up on the streets, took his GED, and ended up at MIT. Most of you reading this book will not fall into this category, and in any event those kinds of life experiences and accomplishments cannot be manufactured or executed over the couple of months or years in which you're thinking about applying to law school.

If Your Numbers Are in the Mushy Middle

If you're in that 70 percent of files that don't have exceptionally high or low numbers—if you're hovering somewhere around the medians, or if you're what we call a "mixed predictor" (a higher LSAT score coupled with a lower GPA, or vice versa)—your job is the hardest. Your job is to distinguish yourself from the pack, which is essentially a marketing exercise. Nobody in the pure and unsullied academic world (including admissions officers) would characterize it that way, but that's basically what your job is: to sell yourself. The shorthand I like to use is the "wow factor"— that je ne sais quoi in an application that makes an admissions officer want you over all the other people in the mushy middle. There is no one way to make them think "wow," because applicants all bring a different balance sheet to the table, with a different mix of assets and liabilities. What distinguishes the successful applicants from the unsuccessful is a coherent, considered marketing strategy that makes the most of their assets, diffuses the impact of their liabilities, and communicates their personalities. That's much easier said than done, I know. The rest of this book will help you do that, and you should also take a look at the Brainstorm Questionnaire I use with my clients to help us figure out their personal balance sheets and their best marketing strategies—you'll find a copy in Appendix A.

Keep in mind that if you're in the mushy middle, there are some common mistakes that are likely to land you in the rejection pile (or, as many applicants call it, the "ding pile") right off the bat. Don't make it *easy* for them to reject you.

- Don't let any typos slip through the cracks, and don't rely on spell-check. If you find a typo after you submitted your application, call up the admissions office, be very nice to the person who answers the phone, and ask if you can substitute a page in your file. If your file hasn't already been sent off for evaluation, they'll probably let you. If you find more than one typo in your essay, go ahead and substitute the whole essay. If you can't substitute that page or that essay, go to your Happy Place with the knowledge that the odds are they won't even notice. (If, on the other hand, you find multiple typos dispersed throughout your application, you look bad no matter what, whether you leave the mess as is or ask to substitute the entire thing. Don't let that be you.)

- Cutting and pasting is dangerous. Don't tell Stanford how badly you want to attend Cornell. It happens all the time, and it's so very sad.

- Don't mistreat anyone on the phone. Deans of admissions answer phones, too, and frontline office staff can get you blacklisted and make your life miserable in many other ways. They work hard and deserve your respect.

■ Follow instructions to the letter. Read the application instructions carefully, and read the application form carefully. If they tell you not to refer to a résumé instead of filling out the employment section, don't. If they tell you not to submit attachments, don't. If they tell you to use the Law School Data Assembly Service (LSDAS) recommendation forms (a standardized recommendation form offered by LSAC, the Law School Admission Council), do. If they tell you not to call to check on the status of your application, don't. If they ask you to write an essay on why you want to attend their law school, don't send them the essay about your passion for bridge that you're sending everyone else. And if they give you any specific instructions that contradict what I say here, follow those instead. Remember that law is one of the more detail-oriented professions on earth, and admissions officers look for people who demonstrate exceptional attention to detail. If you make silly mistakes as an applicant, you're telling admissions officers that *even at your best*, you still mess up the details.

The next few chapters delve into the nonnumbers parts of the application—the essay, the résumé, recommendations, and addenda—and explain how you can make the most of your strengths and mitigate your weaknesses in each. Here, we'll first tackle the LSAT and the GPA, and deal with some preliminary questions.

WHY DO THE NUMBERS MATTER SO MUCH?

Applicants are always howling and whining about how the numbers matter too much, but they have only themselves to blame. Admissions officers don't want to be slaves to the numbers, either. They know that the LSAT is a limited tool for predicting how someone will do in law school, let alone as a lawyer, and that your GPA, as a raw number, means nothing without taking into account where you went to school, what you majored in, and how hard your classes were, let alone what other responsibilities and accomplishments you have to show for during your college years. And every year they have to turn away people they *love* just because of low numbers.

So why do the numbers matter so much? Because the famous *U.S. News & World Report* rankings evaluate law schools in large part based on these medians, and the overwhelming majority of applicants decide where to go to law school based on those rankings. I see this all the time—applicants who pick one law school over another because it's ranked just one spot or two higher. Until applicants become better consumers and do their own research, this situation will not change. If applicants didn't care so much about those rankings, law schools wouldn't care so much about your numbers. It's that simple.

In relying so heavily on the rankings, you do yourself a disservice in other ways as well. Take a look at the rankings criteria sometime. Those postgraduation employment statistics? They don't distinguish between the law school graduate who clerks for Sandra Day O'Connor and the graduate who serves lattes at Starbucks. Those GPA stats? They don't distinguish between a 3.5 in Interior Design from Chico State and a 3.5 in Astrophysics from Caltech (and by that I don't mean to disparage interior designers or Chico State, but I do mean to point out that the number alone fails to convey a lot of important context). The rankings give weight to how many books take up space in the library (totally irrelevant in this day and age), and reward schools that generate and then deny as many applications as possible (creating a huge incentive to encourage applications from people who don't stand a chance).

That last point is important. You'll *never* hear an admissions officer tell you that you don't stand a chance, or that you shouldn't apply. If they reject you, they'll never tell you that you shouldn't *re*apply. They'll tell you that even if your numbers stink, you can basically still write your way into law school. I appreciate the pressure they're under—it's their job to generate as many applications as possible—but it's just not realistic to say that you can write your way into law school if your numbers aren't in the ballpark. The numbers matter much more than admissions officers let on. Applicants sugarcoat themselves in their applications—that's the nature of the beast—but

(continued on next page)

don't forget that law schools sugarcoat the application process, too.

More important, the rankings don't factor in some things that really do matter to many applicants, like the per capita placement rate for federal appellate and Supreme Court clerkships, or the schools' reputations among the top law firms, or the quality of teaching and access to professors. (To get a sense of those rankings, take a look at the Leiter Rankings at www.utexas.edu/law/faculty/bleiter/rankings). I could go on, but you get the idea.

Don't get me wrong—I'm not ideologically opposed to rankings. I think they serve a purpose in helping people get a very general sense of the caliber of different law schools in the grand scheme of things. I've met plenty of applicants who really didn't know that Cornell Law School and Brooklyn Law School are very different "products," or that the University of Chicago Law School isn't some commuter school. By all means—pay attention to the criteria *you* care about. Just don't assume you care about the same things as the august editors of *U.S. News & World Report*. Law school applicants are about to spend a small fortune on an investment that will determine their future careers, and yet they are some of the most ignorant consumers around. They do more research when trying to decide between a Honda CR-V and a Toyota RAV4 than they do when picking a law school. You owe yourself more than that.

THE LSAT

I know, the LSAT stinks, but for now it's your problem and you need to deal with it head-on. According to the LSAC, the organization that develops and administers the LSAT, the test is supposed to "measure skills that are considered essential for success in law school: the reading and comprehension of complex texts with accuracy and insight; the organization and management of information and the ability to draw reasonable inferences from it; the ability to think critically; and the analysis and evaluation of the reasoning and arguments of others." More specifically, it aims to predict how a person will do in his first year of law school. LSAC employs a whole stable of statisticians who examine historical LSAT and law school data a zillion different ways, and their data suggest a strong correlation between a person's LSAT score and her first-year law school grades. (The combination of a person's undergraduate GPA and LSAT turns out to be an even better predictor of first-year grades.) So as much as you may hate the test, it turns out that it does a pretty good job at what it purports to measure. Law school admissions officers understand that it doesn't reveal anything about your motivation or work ethic or values or emotional intelligence, and that it doesn't predict how you're going to do as a lawyer out in the real world. They look to other parts of your application—your undergraduate record, your work and life experience, and your recommendations— to gauge those other qualities.

What Do Admissions Officers Think
of Multiple LSAT Scores?

Many applicants are tempted to take the test as a dry run
to see how they do. Big mistake! Your multiple scores show
up on your LSAT Score Report, which is sent to all the law
schools you apply to. Many schools, like Berkeley, average
your scores, which means that you would have to do substantially better your second time to raise your average by
any significant amount. And, of course, you risk seeing your
second score dragging your average *down*. Other schools,
like Michigan, take all your scores into consideration, as
well as their average. Only a minority of schools, like Northwestern, will take your highest score. As a matter of strategy, you're better off taking the LSAT only once, with
preparation, and doing it right the first time.

The odds are also against you if you think you can do
substantially better a second or third time. LSAC publishes
statistics on the success of multiple-test takers, and the re-
sults are not encouraging. The data show that people tend to
improve their scores by only a point or two, and a good number of people actually do worse.

Say, for example, that you scored a 143 the first time,
and you're feeling confident that you can score in the 160s if
you set your mind to it. Consider these odds though: Of the
people who were retaking the test in the 2001–2002 season
after having scored a 143 previously, only one person out of
981 scored in the 160–169 range (a mere 0.1 percent!), and
none scored in the 170–180 range. In contrast, a whopping

98 out of 981 (10 percent) scored lower than they had the first time, i.e., in the 120–139 range. If you have a score that you're not happy with, you can go to a chart in the *LSAT & LSDAS Registration and Information Book* (available online at www.lsac.org) to look up the odds.

If you do decide to take it more than once, your second score is considerably better than the first, *and* you have a good reason why law schools should discount or disregard the lower score (say, you've taken several courses in formal logic in between tests and that training helped you boost your score), you can write an addendum to your application explaining to admissions officers why they should do so. If you don't have that good a reason for the jump, you should let the higher score speak for itself. (See Chapter 6 for more guidance.)

Should I Take a Commercial LSAT Prep Course?

When I was an admissions officer, there was a weird kind of tacit gag rule in the admissions community regarding commercial prep courses. The official line was: "You don't need a prep course to do well on the LSAT, and we don't recommend that you take one." That's just silly. The fact is that the LSAT is a very learnable test. That doesn't mean you have to take a $1,000 course—you might be the kind of person who has the discipline to work through the many LSAT prep books on the market. But don't kid yourself: You should prepare for this test, and there is an art to taking it. If you wanted to budget $1,000 to spend on any way you could to improve your admissions chances, you'd get great bang for your buck spending it on boosting your LSAT score.

Why are admissions officers so reticent about acknowledging the "learnability" of the LSAT? They don't like the fact that they put so much weight on a test that can be "learned" for $1,000. They don't like the fact that people who can spend $1,000 have any kind of advantage in such an important part of the admissions process. And they don't want to endorse for-profit, commercial businesses that cater to those needs, because admissions officers, like people in academia generally, are somewhat suspicious of the for-profit world. And in admissions officers' defense, some test prep companies are just plain bad and a waste of money. Some instructors have never taken the LSAT, and some walked in off the street and applied for a job two hours before standing in front of a prep class. If you decide to take a prep class, pay attention to the details and ask questions before you sign up.

How Do They Interpret LSAT Score Cancellations?

Before you walk out of your LSAT test, and for nine calendar days afterward (as of this printing), you have the option of canceling your score. While your score isn't reported to law schools, admissions officers will get to see that you took the test and canceled your score. Admissions officers understand that bad days can and do happen to everyone, and they won't look askance at a single score cancellation. If you cancel it a second or a third time, though, you start looking like a flake at best. At worst, you look like someone who can't handle the pressure of a half-day test, and they will rightly wonder how you're going to survive law school, let alone the bar exam or legal practice. If you have good reasons for canceling more than once (which is unlikely as a matter of probability, for example, if there's an earthquake during your first test and you have food poisoning during your second test), see Chapter 6 for further tips on how best to convey them to admissions officers.

If your test date is approaching and you know that you won't be ready for it, you can also postpone or cancel your test registration ahead of time. (See www.lsac.org for cancellation deadlines.) If you cancel it ahead of time, that cancellation is *not* reported to law schools. On the other hand, if you don't cancel your test ahead of time and just don't show up, law schools will be notified that you were a no-show. Don't do that. It's bad form, and it reflects poorly on you to admissions officers.

Does Anyone Really Care About the LSAT Writing Sample?

Yes! The LSAT writing samples don't need to be as polished or beautiful as your application essay, but too large a discrepancy between the caliber of your essay and the caliber of your writing sample will raise red flags. Admissions officers will suspect that you had so much help on your essay that it's really no longer your own (a no-no), or they'll wonder if your ability to write under time pressure is so deficient that you'll have trouble writing law school exams and meeting tough court deadlines. They also pay special attention to the writing samples of applicants whose native language is not English, because they want to make sure that their mastery of written English is sufficient to succeed in law school and beyond.

What Do I Do If I Think My Disability Will Interfere with My LSAT Test Taking?

If you have a disability, whether it's a physical disability or a learning disability, you should be tested by professionals and have your disability documented so that you can petition LSAC for testing accommodations. (See www.lsac .org for more information on testing accommodations.) Accommodations can range from extra time on the test to breaks between sections to having a reader read the questions to you. Of course LSAC doesn't grant every request, but it's certainly an avenue you should explore if you have a disability.

When Should I Take the LSAT?

Ideally, you'll take it no later than the June before you apply, but the latest you should take it is in October of the fall in which you are applying. I recommend taking it in June because that way, if you're not happy with your score and want to retake the test in October, you'll still have plenty of time to get your applications in nice and early. If you wait until October to take it for the first time, your only option is to retake it in December, and your file won't be complete until late December at the earliest—not a wise strategy (more on that on page 41).

On the other hand, you should not take the LSAT more than three years before you plan to apply. Schools have different policies about the age of LSAT scores they'll accept, but most fall between three and five years.

YOUR GPA

As I explained previously, the raw number of your GPA is an absolutely worthless piece of information when taken out of context. When you send your transcripts to LSAC for processing (as every applicant is required to do in order to apply to most law schools), LSAC runs its own nuanced analysis of your grades and sends it to law schools on their Academic Summary Report (with copies of the transcripts themselves attached). And when I say "nuanced," I'm not kidding. Because nearly every law school applicant across the country has had to run his transcript and LSAT information through LSAC since at least 1976, LSAC has a wealth of data that allows admissions officers to compare law school applicants to one another. LSAC slices and dices your transcripts in very interesting ways—bear with me, because you'll learn a lot about how admissions officers interpret your grades with the help of your Academic Summary Report. This is especially important information if you haven't graduated from college yet and you're making choices about course selection and workload. Here are some of the highlights:

Institutions Attended The Report lists every post-secondary (i.e., post–high school) institution you attended, what degree you earned there (if any), when it was awarded, what your major was at your degree-granting college, and whether you attended those institutions at the undergraduate or graduate level. If your undergraduate transcript includes any notes for a particular year like dean's list, academic honors, credits from study-abroad programs, or academic probation, those things are noted as well.

Your College's LSAT Score Distribution LSAC also compiles all the LSAT data it has for your degree-granting college going back to 1991 and shows how law school applicants from your college have fared on the LSAT. The score distributions allow admissions officers to get a sense of how competitive your school is, on the assumption that a school where most of its law school applicants score well on the LSAT is a tougher school than one where only a small percentage scores well on the LSAT.

For example, it might show that 23 percent of law school applicants from your college have scored in the 95th percentile or higher, and that another 10 percent scored between the 90th and 94th percentiles. Those numbers would suggest that your school is much more competitive than a college where 0 percent of its law school applicants scored in the 95th percentile or higher, and only 2 percent scored between the 90th and 94th percentiles.

Your College's GPA Distribution   The same kind of percentage distribution is shown for the GPAs of your school's law school applicants, but only for the years in which you attended. That distribution gives admissions officers a sense of how much grade inflation there was at your school when you were there. For example, if the Report shows that 36 percent of your school's applicants had GPAs above 3.6, that suggests that your school had an easier grading curve than a school where only 12 percent of its law school applicants had GPAs above 3.6. Since a school's law school applicants are not necessarily representative of its undergraduates as a whole, law school admissions officers don't read *too* much into those data, but the information is very helpful in comparing law school applicants from one college to law school applicants from another college.

Your College Grades   The Report shows a grid breaking down your undergraduate transcripts year by year. (It will show a column for the years you attended graduate school, but the grid does not summarize any graduate transcripts— admissions officers have to analyze graduate transcripts on their own. The same is true for transcripts from foreign schools.)

■ For each year and each college, it shows the average LSAT score of that college's law school applicants for the three most recent years you attended, and it shows the number of law school applicants from which that average was calculated. That's just another twist on the information about LSAT score distributions (discussed above) that allows admissions officers to get a sense of the competitiveness of your school, and also to show them whether your college sends a lot of people to law school or only a few.

■ For each year, it lists the number of semester credit hours you earned at each school, revealing to admissions officers changes in your workload over time.

■ For each year, it shows your GPA for all grades earned during that year. It also tracks your cumulative GPA over time. That allows admissions officers to see, for example, if your grades improved over time (suggesting that your earlier grades are not as representative of your current capabilities), or if you had a bad year amid otherwise great grades (suggesting that the bad year was really an exception).

■ For each year, it shows the percentage of law school applicants from that school whose GPAs were below yours, and it also shows the average GPA for law school applicants from your college. While that information doesn't let admissions officers compare you to all your college peers, they can at least gauge how you compare academically to other law school applicants from your college.

If you received a W (withdraw), F (fail), NP (no pass), NC (no credit), or I (incomplete) in any of your courses, you should be aware that LSAC may not treat them the same way as your school does for GPA purposes.

▣ LSAC includes the credits for those courses in the calculation of your GPA (that is, it treats you as having earned an F or a zero) if your school indicates that you attempted the credits *and* your school considers the grade to be punitive. In that case, even if your *school* doesn't include those credits when it calculates your GPA on its transcript, your Academic Summary Report will. The Report also treats a "no credit" grade as an F, even if your school doesn't consider it punitive.

▣ If you repeat a course, all grades and credits that you earn for that course are factored into the Report GPA calculations as long as the course units and grades appear on your transcript. So even if your school overlooks your first attempt in its GPA calculations, LSAC won't.

Admissions officers have all that information about your grades before they even turn to the next page and look at the actual transcripts. Transcripts themselves can be very oblique. Many schools abbreviate course names beyond recognition, and they don't always clarify the level of difficulty of various courses. Most transcripts give no information about the grading curve for your individual classes—that's why admissions officers love Dartmouth transcripts, because they list the average grade for each class. Dartmouth is the exception, though. Most school transcripts aren't nearly that helpful.

The bottom line is that admissions officers analyze your grades very carefully. If you think your transcript undersells you—if it doesn't, for example, make clear that those economics classes you took were graduate-level courses, or that "IND PROJ" was really a senior thesis, or if you want admissions officers to understand that there were external circumstances that compromised your ability to succeed during your sophomore year—you should write an addendum. (See Chapter 6.)

Are Some Schools Known for Grade Inflation or for Lack of Grade Inflation?

All the Ivy League schools, as well as Stanford and Yeshiva, are notorious among law school admissions officers for their grade inflation. The administrations of Stanford, Princeton, and Harvard have publicly declared war on grade inflation, but they haven't won those battles yet. Schools that are known, on the other hand, for their tough grading curves are Reed, Harvey Mudd, Swarthmore, Chicago, Johns Hopkins, Caltech, Georgia Tech, and the military academies. (To give you some idea, not a single person in Chicago's class of 2004 graduated with a 4.0 average.) Admissions officers are also familiar with some of the more unusual transcripts, like those from Santa Cruz and St. John's, which don't use conventional grades but provide written evaluations instead.

If you attended a college that does not engage in grade inflation, and it is not obvious that your GPA is actually on the high end for your school, the burden is on you to communicate that to admissions officers, either in your résumé, in a recommendation, or in an addendum.

How Are My Community College Grades Evaluated?

Some high school seniors take classes at a local community college to challenge themselves beyond their high school curriculum. When you apply to law school, you will be required to submit those community college transcripts to LSAC. If you blew off your community college classes your senior year, they will drag down your GPA as calculated by LSAC, but an admissions officer will be able to see that you took those classes before starting college and will most likely not weight them as heavily as the classes you took after high school.

Other applicants have community college grades because they started out at a community college after high school and then transferred to a four-year program. Those grades will be scrutinized just like any other college grades.

Are There Particular Majors That Are Assumed to Be Difficult or Fluffy?

Admissions officers understand that students majoring in mathematics, the hard sciences, and engineering are typically

subjected to much tougher grading curves than students majoring in the humanities. There are also majors that are assumed to enjoy lenient grading unless you present evidence
to the contrary: Sociology, languages, Communications, visual and performing arts, any "identity politics" majors like
Women's Studies or African American Studies, Journalism,
and any class that involves watching Eminem videos or
studying the Beatles. There are also certain majors at specific schools that are well known to admissions officers as
relatively fluffy in terms of grading, like Social Studies at
Harvard. Of course these are generalizations, and if, say, Sociology at Princeton is actually a very rigorous program (as
I'm told it is), then you should look at the techniques I suggest in Chapters 4 and 6 for educating admissions officers
about your program.

On a related note, law schools typically prefer liberal
arts majors (and here I include math and science) over preprofessional majors like Business, Accounting, or Pre-Law.
The higher up the food chain a law school is, the stronger
the bias against preprofessional programs. Admissions officers believe (whether rightly or wrongly) that a well-rounded
grounding in the liberal arts offers much better training for
law school than a preprofessional program, and pre-law programs in particular bear almost no relationship to the kinds
of things one learns in law school. If you're neck-deep in
your preprofessional major and can't easily switch, make
sure to bulk up on some traditional liberal arts classes, like
history, English, or economics.

Note that engineering, a preprofessional major, is the exception because there is such high demand for that background in the field of patent law, where people with science and engineering backgrounds tend to rule the roost.

Do Admissions Officers Take Graduate Work into Consideration?

Even though LSAC doesn't provide analyses of graduate school transcripts on the Academic Summary Report, admissions officers do take your graduate work into consideration. The nature of the graduate work will influence how seriously they take those grades. For example, almost no one gets bad grades in a PhD program in the humanities, so a 4.0 there wouldn't be treated as a superstar grade. (Master's degrees can be a different story—grading practices vary more widely than they do in PhD programs, and you should educate admissions officers about your program.)

OTHER BIG-PICTURE ADMISSIONS QUESTIONS

How Does Affirmative Action Work?

This topic made it all the way to the U.S. Supreme Court, and most applicants are intensely curious about how affirmative action works. If you self-identify as African American, Latino, or Native American, you will find it easier to get into the top schools. Why? Because there are disproportionately fewer of those minorities with the numbers schools are looking for than there are among nonminority applicants. There are several competing theories about the reasons for that discrepancy, but for the purposes of this book, it matters simply that the discrepancy exists, and that the discrepancy affects your admissions chances. In some years, it is not unusual for admission officers to dip up to ten points lower on the LSAT for a member of one of these minority groups compared to the numbers they would expect from white applicants, to the point where minorities are often accepted with numbers that would sink white applicants. (There's a bit of wiggle room on the GPA side, but not nearly as much as with the LSAT.) Admissions officers are accountable to their law school administrations, their professors, their students, and their alumni for putting together a class that won't embarrass the school in terms of race distributions, and they monitor their minority offers and acceptances very carefully to make sure the incoming class doesn't have too few of those minorities.

And "white," for the purposes of law school admissions, covers pretty much everyone else, whether it's South Asians or Iraqi Americans or Ashkenazi Jews. That frustrates many people to no end, and admissions officers receive constant complaints from applicants on the subject. But that's unlikely to change any time soon, because admissions officers don't track—and are not looking to boost—the percentage of South Asians or Iraqi Americans or Ashkenazi Jews, because they are not accountable to their constituents for those numbers. Applicant complaints are unlikely to change that. Also understand that admissions officers do not set their schools' affirmative action policies—their bosses, the deans of the law schools, do.

In some states, public schools have been barred, either by referendum or by judicial fiat, from applying different admissions standards to different races. For example, public schools in California and Texas started asking applicants about their socioeconomic status rather than their race, although the University of Texas system is now reverting to its previous race-based affirmative action policies following recent Supreme Court rulings.

Public schools also give preference to in-state applicants. For example, the University of Washington limits its nonresident enrollment to 30 percent of the student body, and the University of Florida imposes a limit of 10 percent. The states all prescribe their own residency requirements for admissions purposes, and individual schools will share with you what they are.

Women used to have an affirmative action advantage in admissions, but the numbers have shifted enough that women now make up a slight majority at many law schools. They no longer receive admissions preferences unless a school is trying to work its way up to 50 percent representation.

One question I hear from time to time is the following: How black/Latino/Native American do I have to be to check that box? Most people aren't 100 percent anything these days (if they ever were). One really interesting aspect to affirmative action in practice is that minority status is self-reported.

Schools don't ask—and don't really want to know—just how ethnic a self-reported minority applicant really is. For example, I remember an applicant who was one-eighth African American, and she debated whether to check off that box in order to enjoy the rewards of minority status in the admissions process. When she called admissions offices to find out what their standards were for classifying people as minorities, she learned that no school wants to go on the record about that, because a formal policy (A half? A quarter? One drop?) would be much too awkward. Plus, as I discussed above, schools have an incentive to boost their minority numbers, so they don't want to discourage people from self-identifying as minorities.

The bottom line is that admissions officers don't want to be policing people's ethnicity, and it's not surprising that a lot of applicants exploit that discomfort. I don't know of any outright fraud involving someone with zero claim to a certain ethnicity, but I have come across applicants who take advantage of a very tenuous connection, and at this time there are no repercussions for them.

How Much of an Advantage Do Legacies Have?

"Legacies" are the children and other close relatives of alumni. In my experience, your relatives would have to have given a gift in the seven figures to influence your admissions chances at a top law school in a meaningful way. However, even alumni and family connections who haven't donated big bucks can and do help if you're borderline, because schools love the idea of a whole family having warm and fuzzy feelings for their alma mater in the hopes that the family nostalgia will translate into a hefty gift down the road. Still, it is not common for a law school dean or a university president to insist on the admission of a law school applicant who is not at least in the running. Professors might also put in a good word for an applicant, but they, too, tend to show deference to the professional judgment of the admissions officer. Nobody cares, as a matter of principle, if there are too few legacies in any given class, and nobody tries to make sure that there are at least X number of legacies represented every year. It really depends on the school's relationship to the particular alumnus, and whether the school can afford to tick him off.

Does It Matter When in the Application Season I Apply?

If there's only one thing you take away from this book, it's this: *Apply as early in the application season as possible.* Admissions officers generally don't start reading files until just after Thanksgiving, so you should aim to have your application complete by Thanksgiving at the latest. And by "complete," I mean totally signed, sealed, and delivered, with no outstanding pieces. Why does applying early matter so much? A couple of reasons:

■ *Application flow:* Early in the season, admissions officers take more time to read files than when they're crushed by the deluge of applications submitted closer to the deadline. Their minds are fresher and their focus is sharper. They have more time to get to know you, and that usually works in your favor.

■ *Human psychology:* Think of it this way: The first time you come across a one-legged ice-skater, you're blown away by her resilience and chutzpah and zest for life. The second or third time you come across a one-legged ice-skater during that admissions season, you're going to think, "Nice kid, but I've already admitted a one-legged ice-skater, and I'm looking for something different." However special you think you are, you'll seem a lot less special later in the season when admissions officers have seen thousands of other applications.

■ *Signaling:* By submitting your application early, you signal to the admissions officer that you're on the ball— that you're organized and don't wait until the last second. You also signal that you're very interested in that school—lots of people send out another round of applications as deadlines approach because they panic and apply to more schools just to be safe.

■ *Money:* Financial aid is distributed on a first-come, first-served basis, and funds may have dried up if you apply late in the season.

■ *Medians:* In the early part of the admissions season, admissions officers admit people because they like them.

In the later part of the admissions season, they admit people to manage the school's LSAT and GPA medians, so your numbers will matter much more.

Do Early Action and Early Decision Applicants Have an Advantage?

This is a yes-and-no kind of answer. Because the rankings penalize schools for every offer they make that isn't accepted, admissions officers would much rather make an offer to someone they think is going to accept than to someone about whom they're not sure, all else being equal. If you apply to a binding early decision program, you are promising that you'll attend, so that removes any doubt they have about whether you'll accept their offer. Nonbinding early action programs signal your strong interest in the school, which also inures to your benefit but doesn't, of course, signal that you'll definitely attend.

On the other hand, applicants factor in that slight edge when they're deciding when and where to apply, and schools that have offered binding early decision programs have found that their early decision pool tends to be weaker than the regular decision pool, so they end up rolling a lot of those applicants over into the regular decision pool until they have a better sense of what that year's total pool is going to look like.

Note that if you commit to a binding early decision application, you give up practically all your leverage for scholarships. See Chapter 8 for more on that.

How Much Do Recommendations Really Matter?

To be honest, very few recommendations ever changed my mind one way or another. Most of them were positive and bland. The ones that did change my opinion, and changed the admissions outcome, were the small minority that conveyed why an applicant was really special and I'd be a fool not to want him, as well as another small minority that were either overtly negative ("I cannot recommend this person") or, more frequently, that damned applicants with faint praise ("he works very hard" or "she is very nice"). You can find more recommendation tips in Chapter 4.

Does Being an Older Applicant Help Me or Hurt Me?

Admissions officers are happy to receive applications from older students. When they say they're looking to put together a diverse class, they don't just mean diversity in the check-the-box sense. They are trying to put together a class of people who bring different personalities, talents, and life experiences to the table. As I explained to an older applicant in my "Ask Anna" advice column on Vault.com, "Older students who've been out in the real world raising their families, paying their taxes, refinancing their homes, battling their school districts, and finessing their way through office politics offer a fantastic and necessary counterbalance to the kids who've never filled out a 1040 and still have Che Guevara posters on their walls. When the kiddies raise their hands to wax rhapsodic about 80 percent tax rates and express outrage about body-piercing discrimination in the workplace, you'll be able to inject a nice reality check into the discussion." Use your life experience to your advantage. That said, older applicants should know that, compared to younger applicants, they may face tougher job prospects if the economy is down, even if they're coming from top law schools.

Do They Prefer People Who Have Work Experience? Does It Have to Be Legal Work Experience?

Most law schools will tell you that work experience won't hurt or help you in the admissions process, but I don't think that's accurate in practice. It's only logical that if you do something worthwhile after college, whether as a junior analyst at an investment bank or as a volunteer at a refugee camp in Rwanda, those experiences will make you a more attractive applicant than you would have been without that real-world experience.

Law schools typically don't care one way or the other if you have *legal* work experience, although I highly recommend that you get your feet wet in a legal job so that you know what you're getting into before applying. It will also give you great insight and credibility when it comes time to explain in your essays why you want to go to law school, not to mention career connections and mentors when you're in the job market after law school.

What If I Want to Explain a Weakness in My Application?

The best place to explain a blemish in your file is an addendum. Don't use up valuable space in your personal

statement to explain why you flunked French Deconstruc-
tionism or how you had mono your sophomore year or how
your LSAT proctor called time too early. (See Chapter 6 for
advice on addenda.)

If I Have a Criminal Record,
Should I Bother to Apply?

Law schools have admitted convicted murderers and
drug dealers, so a criminal record in and of itself doesn't
stand in the way of your law school dreams. However, applicants with criminal records should contact their state bar associations before they apply to law school to find out
whether their records will prevent them from becoming
members of the state bar. If the state bar gives you the go-
ahead, then you can worry about winning over the admissions committee. (See Chapter 6 for suggestions.)

As a more general matter, if you did some unsavory
things in your past, you must disclose them if asked to do so
on the application form. Most applications ask about felony
and misdemeanor *convictions*; others ask more broadly
about *charges.* You will also be expected to disclose any disciplinary problems you had in college and grad school. *If in
doubt, disclose.* Even if you're not inclined to do so as an
ethical matter, self-interest also dictates honesty. As tempting as it may be to fudge, dissemble, obfuscate, or lie, if law
schools find out that you weren't honest on your applications, they can retract their offers and even kick you out of
law school. And if the state bar finds out, it can prevent you

from practicing law for the rest of time, which is a real bummer if you've just spent three years in law school and are up to your eyeballs in student debt.

TRUE STORIES

Once, while reading an LSDAS Report (the master report that LSAC sends over with an applicant's LSAT scores and transcripts), I noticed that the font in the bottom corner looked just the slightest bit off. Ordinarily, one wouldn't expect any formatting variation from report to report, because they all get spit out by the same computers at LSAC. So I picked up the phone and called LSAC to confirm the applicant's LSAT scores. You can imagine my surprise when they informed me that they had not received a request to send us an LSDAS Report for that applicant, and that we shouldn't have a copy yet. Lo and behold, when the real LSDAS Report arrived, the LSAT score was lower by a good ten points, and the grades on his transcripts were also considerably less stellar.

I have to hand it to the guy. He must have spent night after night in our admissions office, cutting and pasting and copying from other files and getting the paper and font just so and making sure his "file" ended up in the right cabinet. He even figured out the cryptic shorthand we

(continued on next page)

used for listing basic data on the applicant file tabs. He
was masterful, but he'll have to stick to forgery and breaking and entering, because he won't be practicing law. Ever.

I also remember an applicant who plagiarized his essay
from an article in an Ivy League alumni magazine that an
admissions officer happened to receive. Well, duh! I still
wonder if that applicant was, deep down, trying to sabo-
tage himself. Either that, or he just wasn't the sharpest tool
in the shed. This kind of stuff happens often enough that
admissions officers are pretty good at smelling a rat. That
doesn't mean they catch everyone, but be forewarned that
the odds are against you and the repercussions are severe.

I Received a Letter from a Law School Encouraging Me to Apply. What's That All About?

Those letters are called CRS letters, short for Candidate
Referral Service. When you register to take the LSAT, you
are asked to indicate whether you would like LSAC to forward your information to law schools that want to recruit
people who meet certain profiles. For example, they might
ask LSAC for lists of people who score above a 165 on the
LSAT and have a GPA higher than 3.6, or they might ask for
a list of all self-reported black or gay test takers in their
state. Usually there are two different kinds of CRS letters:
the ones that invite you to apply and the ones that also offer
to waive your application fee.

The benign explanation for this practice is that law schools want to introduce themselves to promising applicants who might not otherwise know about them. The less benign explanation is that they need to generate as many applications as possible to improve their place in the rankings. Those letters will always say that you should not interpret them as any guarantee that you will be accepted, and you should believe them. Personally, if I were an applicant who had been solicited by a law school that then pocketed my application fee and turned me down, I would be pretty ticked, and I don't understand why law schools risk that loss of goodwill. Some schools are just very aggressive when it comes to improving their spot in the rankings. If a school offers you a fee waiver, of course, you have nothing to lose but your time.

Should I Submit My Application Electronically or in Hard Copy?

LSAC makes it pretty easy to submit your applications electronically through their website. Unless a law school instructs you to submit your application one way and not the other, you should do whatever is easier for you. Here's a real downside to submitting your applications online, though: For some reason, even though you may be uploading your essays and résumés to the LSAC server with beautiful formatting, many times the formatting gets stripped out in transit and your documents end up being downloaded by the law schools as big, ugly, unformatted blocks of text. That's not too problematic where your essays are concerned, but it

does make your résumés impossible to read. If you do decide
to submit electronically, you should still send a hard copy of
your résumé (or anything else with a lot of formatting) just
in case—just make sure to label them in your cover letter as
formatted but otherwise unchanged copies of their electronic counterparts. And if you submit your applications in
hard copy, don't pinch pennies on shipping. Send them by
FedEx, UPS, or U.S. Postal Service Express Mail with deliv-
ery confirmation so that you can be sure they'll get there
(sadly, that's not a foregone conclusion with first-class mail)
and so that you can confirm when they arrived.

Are Applicants Penalized for Reapplying?

Admissions officers welcome reapplications, both because they like to receive as many applications as possible
for rankings purposes, but also because every year they have
to turn down applicants they like, even love. The applicant
pool changes every year, and it's possible that you could
stack up better against the competition the second time
around.

That being said, when people reapply to law schools, admissions officers expect that something will be different—
and better—about your application, whether it's a higher
LSAT score, another semester's worth of grades, a prestigious fellowship, or a new activity or job. If you submit what
is essentially the same application the following year (usually just six to nine months after your rejection letter, if
you're heeding my advice and applying early the second

time), admissions officers will wonder why you expect them to admit you this time if you didn't make the cut last time.

Even though reapplication is an option, you're much better off applying only once, when you're in peak form (see page 131 about waiting until you can submit the strongest application). That's because your first application doesn't go away. It stays in your file, and admissions officers will compare the new one to the old one. And there are some things you can't undo (for example, if you asked the wrong person for a recommendation and he wrote unflattering things about you). You're better off doing it right the first time.

A final note: This whole book is dedicated to helping you do the best you can with the parts of the application process you can control. But there are many things that you can't control, and you have to adopt a bit of a Zen attitude about those things. Deans of admissions are accountable to a lot of constituents whom they have to keep happy: they have to keep those medians up for the rankings; they have to admit enough minorities; they have to field requests from deans and professors and students and alums who all have their pet causes and projects and friends and relatives; they have to predict how many people are likely to accept their offers so that they don't end up extending too many (because they wouldn't have enough seats, housing, or teaching staff for the extra students) or too few (because many schools would lose a million dollars in projected revenue for a shortage of just eleven students); they have to make many more financial aid offers than will ultimately be accepted, and they risk promising people money that they won't end up having in their budget if more people than expected accept; they have to make sure they have enough students from different parts of the country and different kinds of colleges. The list goes on and on and on. If you receive a rejection letter that tells you not to take it personally, don't.

CHAPTER 3

Bring Tears—of Joy!—to Their Eyes: The Application Essay

If you're lying awake at night wondering how you're going to tackle your essay, you can take some small comfort in the fact that *every* applicant hates this part. Not only do you have to contend with garden-variety writer's block, but on top of that, most law schools don't give you much guidance on what they're looking for in an essay. Don't fret! Follow these rules and you'll produce an essay that admissions officers will love to read.

The first thing you need to know is that most law school essay questions fall into one of two categories: the open-ended question asking you to write about anything that might help the admissions committee make its decision (what I call the "personal statement"), and the more pointed question asking you to discuss why you're applying to law school (what I call the "statement of purpose"). You'll probably end up having to write each of these essays for different applications, so I've put together a checklist of tips to follow for each essay type. Many law schools also give you an opportunity to write an optional diversity essay, which I discuss on page 89.

THE PERSONAL STATEMENT

Why do admissions officers ask for this type of essay? In a perfect world, every admissions officer could get to know you over a couple of beers. But we don't live in a perfect world, so think of this essay as that kind of friendly heart-to-heart with the admissions officer. The best essays I read always made me think, "I really *like* this person—I would love to run into her in the halls every day for the next three years." It didn't hurt if I also concluded, "She's really smart," or, "She's so accomplished," but that's the purpose of an applicant's transcripts, résumé, and recommendations, not her personal statement. Most applicants waste this opportunity by presenting sides of themselves that they already show off elsewhere in the application. The other important intangible I looked for was diversity—and not just the check-the-box kind. I wanted each class to have a balance of different personality types, ages, professional and academic histories, and geographic and socioeconomic backgrounds. So give serious thought to what sides of yourself you want to present, and where in the application you're going to present them. This is essentially a marketing exercise, and you have to figure out how you're going to position yourself as an applicant.

Good Topics

So how do you find a topic that allows you to reveal something important about yourself in three pages or less? Here are five techniques that will help you generate good topics.

Technique #1: Assume No Knowledge Professional athletes and people recovering from brain aneurysms always have interesting stories to tell in their application essays, but I've found that more average folks have a tougher time finding compelling things to say about themselves. What you need to understand is that while your life might seem boring to you (you live it every day, after all), admissions officers probably have no idea what it's like being you. They don't necessarily know what it's like to grow up judging chickens at 4-H fairs in a small town in Indiana, or what it's like to do your best thinking while gazing at miles of city traffic lights from your fire escape, or what it's like working in an ailing fishing community in Massachusetts. *Everyone* has something interesting to say about where he comes from. And if an admissions officer turns out to come from the same background, so much the better! You'll have built instant rapport with him. In either case, assume that admissions officers know nothing about you. Take a look at the essay called "Morris 405" in Appendix B—it shows us very effectively what it's like to be a classical musician and what it's like to be a cashier at a diner.

Technique #2: Play Against Type   Because admissions officers have so little time to spend on each file, they have to make all kinds of assumptions about applicants. That doesn't make them bad people; they just have to make quick decisions with imperfect information. They might be surprised, for example, to learn that a lab scientist has great people skills, that a communications major has hard quantitative skills, or that a Division I football player is also an expert on Ancient Greek vases. Sometimes those assumptions can be unfair in individual cases, but rather than getting worked up about them, you should figure out what assumptions people will make about you and use them to your advantage. Playing against type makes an admissions officer slow down, sit up, and take notice.

Most people have a pretty good idea of the kinds of stereotypes that apply to them—high school and college students are brutal at stereotyping, after all. If you're worried that admissions officers will assume you have no people skills, for example, emphasize those skills in your résumé and pick an essay topic that highlights those skills. Maybe you haven't led a sports team to victory with your locker room speeches, but I've seen people show off their people skills by distinguishing themselves as resident dormitory advisers, holding squabbling research teams together, or starting student organizations from scratch. One of my favorite essays that played against type came from an ardent environmentalist who had chosen to highlight his pragmatism and business savvy by recounting his success in helping local businesses find cost-effective ways to lower their utility bills. I had gotten used to hearing environmentalist applicants rail against Corporate America, so that essay really got my attention.

Technique #3: Inflection Points At some point in your life, someone must have said something to you that made you rethink your goals, your priorities, or your values. Don't worry if the advice wasn't earth-shattering, or if it wouldn't have meant as much to someone else. Maybe it was just a throwaway line that the speaker has surely forgotten by now but that you remember to this day. This type of essay doesn't even have to involve *words*, just a moment when something or someone made you realize that you wanted to be better or different.

One of the best personal statements I've read started with the thump, thump, thump of a tennis ball hitting the side of a house. The applicant was sitting at home, listening to his brother practice his tennis drills. The applicant had always tried and failed to match his brother as a tennis player, but he finally realized, while listening to the thumping of those tennis balls, that he would have to find and develop his own gifts. He ended up becoming an accomplished photographer. You're probably thinking, "What's so special about that?" The insight itself wasn't so special—most of us have had moments like that—but the applicant wrote his essay in a way that allowed me to step into his shoes for a few minutes. He chose such a small moment to describe, but it was a moment that allowed me to take a focused peek into his life and gave me great insight into his personality. "Morris 405" is also a good example of an inflection essay. In fact, there are several inflection points in that essay: when he immigrated to the United States, when he decided to leave the world of dishwashing behind for a higher education, and when he decided to swap his performing arts education for a math major. Three inflection points is ambitious for a personal statement—one good one will serve you well.

Just make sure that your story is sincere, that the advice or experience genuinely influenced you, and that you chose a different path than you might otherwise have, that you've somehow changed. This kind of experience demonstrates a couple of good things about you as a person: that you are humble and open-minded enough to listen to good advice when you get it, and that you have enough maturity and introspection to think intelligently about the person you want to be.

Take a look at the difference between the "Tattoo Tom" and "Jorge" essays in Appendix B. Both essays are essentially about the same thing: an applicant whose life was apparently changed by a person in unfortunate circumstances. One of the things that makes "Tattoo Tom" work in a way that "Jorge" falls flat is that the "Tattoo Tom" author actually took the time to get to know the person she wrote about. Her essay is very personal and intimate, not an expression of some abstract concept of social justice. In contrast, one doubts whether the other author ever even spoke to Jorge, or that he has anything more than a vague and ham-handed sense of "Gee, it stinks to be poor." The first is a compassionate, thoughtful, and mature applicant, while the second sounds like a spoiled, immature blowhard with delusions of grandeur—surely not the effect he was going for.

The "Jorge" essay also tries to prove too much. The author says, basically, "Because Jorge was poor, I'm going to law school to change the world." In the "Tattoo Tom" essay, on the other hand, we're left to draw our own conclusions about what kind of lawyer the author is going to be, indeed, what kind of human being she is. She doesn't have to tell us that it's her duty to be charitable. We get a strong sense of that from this small sliver of her life, that she's the kind of person who will do the right thing, whether she ends up working at a large law firm or a small legal aid clinic. In contrast, we have no doubt the other writer will forget all about Jorge as soon as he submits his applications.

As a final note on this subject, I will add that if you do write about an important realization, that realization should never be about wanting to become a lawyer. Real people very rarely have great epiphanies about wanting to be lawyers, at least real epiphanies that don't sound hideously trite. And never write "And at that moment I knew..." about anything.

Technique #4: The Tough Decision   Many people have faced at least one really tough decision before they graduated from college. I don't mean the "Should I pick Notre Dame or Boston College?" kind of tough decision. I'm thinking of decisions that require real trade-offs, decisions that taught you something about what it means to be an adult. Some of the better "tough decision" essays I've read dealt with struggles like these:

- Should I pursue a professional acting career or go to college?

- How do I handle a friend who asks me for a recommendation I can't give?

- Should I leave my birth country to emigrate to the United States?

- Should I turn down a substantial gift from my grandparents?

- Should I track down my birth parents?

- Should I break up with the guy whose parents disapprove of our relationship because of my religion?

Don't just describe the conundrum. Explain why it was a difficult choice, what expectations and hopes were wrapped up in it, and the process by which you finally made your decision (or didn't—that's okay, too).

"Tattoo Tom" is a good example. The applicant found herself feeling very uncomfortable as an intern in an Alzheimer's ward, and her interaction with one patient in particular made her uncertain about the right way to conduct herself. She grappled with her discomfort and turned a source of anxiety into a rewarding experience. She faced a choice: She could have taken the easy way out by abandoning her internship or by avoiding the patient who caused her so much grief. But she didn't, and she learned something about herself in the process.

Technique #5: Passion The mark of a good personal statement topic is this: When done badly, it's the worst kind of schlock; but when done right, it communicates something meaningful about who you are. You can't go wrong if you convey your passion for a hobby. One of my favorite essays shared an applicant's passion for reenacting Civil War battles. I had never even considered doing something like that and I can't say he changed my mind, but he successfully communicated his excitement—why it got him out of bed on Saturday mornings to run around in those funny Civil War beards—and the potential schlock factor disappeared. (Well, I guess you could go wrong... you should never write about your passion for anything risqué. No one wants to read about your passion for drinking games or lighting things on fire.) "Morris 405" does a great job at conveying the applicant's passion for math and music. Even if the reader knows nothing of, or doesn't even care for, math or classical music, the essay is a success because it tells us something fundamental about who the author is.

Expressing your passion for a cause is a trickier proposition. Make sure you don't write a Michael Moore or Michael

Savage–style attack piece, regardless of what side of the political fence you sit on ("Why I Hate George Bush" or "Why I Think Illegal Immigrants Are Ruining This Country"). Also, keep in mind that law school admissions officers are overwhelmingly a left-leaning bunch. There are exceptions, of course, but I wouldn't recommend writing about your love for Ronald Reagan or offering your reasoned criticism of affirmative action (which is an article of faith among admissions officers). I would also steer clear of your personal relationship with Jesus or other religious topics, which make some admissions officers squeamish.

Whichever technique you use or topic you pick, keep in mind that most people can't sit down in front of a computer and start writing an intimate portrait of themselves. You should get into the habit of kicking around several ideas at a time, jotting down thoughts onto the back of an envelope or in your PDA as they pop into your head. It's important to leave yourself plenty of time while you're working on your essays—two months is a good window—so that you can let different ideas gestate. In Appendix A, you'll find the Brainstorm Questionnaire, which I use with my counseling clients to help us identify good personal statement topics (among other things). If you spend a couple of hours answering those questions honestly and revisit them periodically, you should be able to generate several good topics.

It's also a good idea to write rough drafts on multiple topics to show to a close friend. It's hard for people to assess someone else's essay in a vacuum, when they have no idea what better alternatives might be buried deep in your head. Give them several choices, and ask them which ones resonate the most strongly and represent you the most faithfully. (This is another reason to start the writing process early.)

FEELING STUCK?

If you're really stumped and need inspiration, invest in a copy of *The Right Words at the Right Time*, edited by Marlo Thomas, a collection of short essays by celebrities about the things people said to them that changed their lives. It's so interesting that many of these famous people reflect on very ordinary experiences that could happen to you or me. Take a look at the essay by Laura Bush, who recalls how she came to love the outdoors after her grandmother told her to look up at the sky during dark summer nights in the Texas desert; or the essay by Jeff Bezos about how he learned that it's harder to be kind than it is to be clever when, as a kid, he made his grandmother cry during a long road trip; or the essay by Jimmy Carter about the elementary schoolteacher who gave him his first copy of Tolstoy and introduced him to the life of the mind. Maybe you're not the first lady or the CEO of Amazon.com or a Nobel Prize–winning president, but this book shows that you don't have to be to tell stories like that.

(continued on next page)

Another excellent resource for helping you brainstorm about essay topics is a book by Lois Daniel called *How to Write Your Own Life Story: The Classic Guide for the Nonprofessional Writer*. It is geared toward people who want to capture their life stories for younger relatives, but the brainstorming process is really the same. It can help you figure out what stories from your background are worth telling, and how to tell them. You'll have to adapt some of the suggested logistics to modern times—for example, the author recommends handwriting your ideas in a three-ring binder, skipping every other line so that you have room to edit your work by hand. I don't know a soul who writes and edits by hand these days, certainly not among people applying to law school. But her suggestions are easily adaptable to laptops and PDAs, and I encourage you to try her brainstorming methods.

Bad Topics

Now that you have some idea of what kinds of topics to choose, let me make your life a little easier by telling you about the most popular topics that usually don't result in great personal statements. I'm not saying that these topics are guaranteed to be awful, just that, based on my experience, I think you're fighting the odds if you choose them.

Bad Topic #1: Why You Want a Law Degree   If admissions officers wanted to know why you're pursuing a law degree, they'd ask you expressly and you'd be writing what I call a statement of purpose, not a personal statement. Most people have lousy reasons for going to law school, so many schools don't even bother asking. The only people who should be discussing their career goals in a personal statement are older applicants pursuing a career change (admissions officers will want to know). This is an especially important tip for current college students who have become disillusioned with their majors (usually pre-med or the hard sciences) and often use their personal statements to explain why their grades were so poor until they decided to become lawyers instead and switched their majors to Poli Sci. That's almost never a good idea for an essay, or even an addendum (more on that in Chapter 6).

Bad Topic #2: A Laundry List of Your Accomplishments   Admissions officers call this essay, disparagingly, the "résumé essay." Other parts of the application already ask you to list your accomplishments, so don't waste the precious real estate of your essay duplicating that information. If one aspect of your academic, extracurricular, or work history tells a meaningful story about you, then you can delve into that one aspect, but keep the focus on you as a person (as opposed to you as a student, club president, or employee) and don't spread yourself too thin. The essay "Korea" in Appendix B is an example of a résumé essay.

Bad Topic #3: An Essay That's Really About Someone Else   Lots of applicants write about people or books that influenced them. Those can be good topics, as I explained earlier, but you must make sure that your essay doesn't turn into an essay about that person or that book. *Your* personality needs to shine through. Applicants never scored any points when the first thought that popped into my head after I finished their essays was, "Wow, I'd really like to admit his grandmother!" or, "I'd really like to read that book!" Take a look at the "Tattoo Tom" essay to see how it's done right. Superficially, the essay might appear to be about Tattoo Tom, but it reveals just as much about the applicant as it does about Tattoo Tom, if not more so. The author does not talk about Tattoo Tom at her own expense. Rather, she uses her relationship with him to elucidate an important lesson she learned. The "Pretty Horses" essay in Appendix B also does a great job of using the author's vacation reading choices to illuminate an important part of his personality.

Bad Topic #4: The Think Piece   With the exception of Yale Law School's notorious 250-word think-piece essay (most of us would call that a paragraph), your essay is not the time or the place to pontificate on abstract ideas or theories, *especially* about the law, a topic that proves endlessly tempting to applicants. I cringed every time an essay started with something like, "The law forces us to examine how social constructs and cultural identities express themselves in rules," or, "I love the art of constructing and deconstructing arguments." Even if you're not writing an entire think piece, you should avoid abstractions as a general matter. For example, if you're writing about your unique background, don't lecture your readers about the meaning of diversity ("Diversity means more than group membership, but rather is formed by personal experiences."). Instead, dive straight into your own story and talk about the interesting things *you* bring to the mix. Admissions officers look to your transcript and recommendations to get a sense of how brainy you are, and any kind of dense, scholarly, or philosophical writing is just too hard for an admissions officer to stomach when she's on file number 3,961. For example, the "Korea" essay in Appendix B uses abstract, scholarly writing that is not appropriate in an application essay ("I have designed my college curriculum to challenge the existing dialectic and engage in a new relativized discourse.").

Don't write your essay about your dissertation topic. If anything, admissions officers want to know that you're more than just another philosophy wonk who couldn't get a job out of grad school. I was always interested to hear the subject of people's academic passions, but for admissions purposes, I was perfectly content to see the title of that senior thesis or dissertation listed on the résumé and to let the recommenders speak to the applicant's academic side.

Also, as a general rule, don't assume that the people reading your file have the same highfalutin education you may have. Some of them are as well read and well educated as the faculty they pass every day in the halls (in fact, some of them will be law professors), but others would never get your sly references to Michel Foucault's theories of deviance or Pascal's *Pensées*. And many admissions officers would never be admitted to the law schools for which they serve as gatekeepers. (That, by the way, has been changing more recently, as law schools have increasingly started hiring their own alums to serve as their admissions officers.)

What other topics did I dread? Some topics are so overused that even when applicants did a bang-up job, I couldn't help but suppress a yawn. The problem wasn't that these essays weren't personal enough but that the applicants had chosen such common topics that they made it impossible to distinguish themselves. So if you've already put together a list of possible essay topics, you can narrow it down by striking these.

Bad Topic #5: Your Trip to Europe, Nepal, or the Amazon I've seen some great travel essays, but they were great only because the applicants were first-rate writers whose work could easily appear in the *New Yorker* or the *Atlantic Monthly*. Of the thousands of travel essays I've read, the first-rate ones were few and far between, because they are so hard to get right. Most end up sounding trite and clichéd, no matter how profound an experience it was for the applicant. For your personal development it's good that you had these experiences, but you face an uphill battle trying to get an admissions officer excited about a travel essay. Unless you are certain of your narrative writing gifts, pick another topic. You can always mention the exotic places you've been in your résumé. An essay that starts off with "My spring break trip to..." is laughable.

If, on the other hand, you've spent a significant amount of time abroad rather than visiting a place on vacation— say, you did a stint in the Peace Corps or you went abroad for your Mormon mission—you should certainly consider writing about that experience. You'll have the credibility to write an authoritative account. And don't chuck a potentially good topic just because the scene is set somewhere abroad. Take a look at the "Pretty Horses" essay. On the surface, it looks like a travel essay, but it's not. It's not "I went here and then I went there and I interacted with people different from me and now I'm a better person." Rather, it's about the applicant's intellectual passion and discovery that he experienced while spending time abroad. The trip and the geography are just an inviting backdrop for his larger story.

Bad Topic #6: Your Passion for Fighting Poverty and Oppression Remember those endangered guppies in the first paragraph of this book? That was an exaggeration, of course. (You knew that, right?) Admissions officers don't read thousands upon thousands of essays about endangered guppies, but a huge number of law school applicants do use their personal statements to explain how committed they are to the public interest, how money doesn't motivate them, and how badly they want to earn a law degree to fight the many and varied evils of the world.

First of all, you should be telling that story in your statement of purpose, not your personal statement. And second, you'll have to forgive admissions officers if they're just a wee bit jaded about these kinds of sentiments. Most of the applicants they admit every year profess this noble goal, but only the tiniest fraction end up in public-interest jobs after graduation. Most of the applicants sending me these essays were applying right out of college, and I knew that they had never held a grown-up job a day in their lives. While I respected the sincerity of their intentions, their lack of real-world work experience always made them sound naive. The only time you should consider this topic is if you have a multiyear track record in public-interest jobs (during or after college) or an application asks you expressly to write about this subject. You can always show off your commitment to the public interest on your résumé. The "Jorge" essay is a great example of what *not* to do. An admissions officer will conclude that the author is either naive and very, very young, or transparently insincere. Neither conclusion helps him as an applicant.

Also, please don't write the ever-popular essay about some horrible injustice that befell your friend or relative and how you want a law degree to see justice done. Very few people really end up doing that, and if you've done little or nothing to help that population or situation thus far, admissions officers will assume you're not going to do it after law school, either.

Bad Topic #7: Excuses   Sometimes life gets in the way of your best efforts and you want admissions officers to understand those circumstances. Maybe your grades dropped while your parents were getting divorced, you had an undiagnosed learning disability, or you had to drop out of school for a while to help your family. It's a good idea to share that information, but don't use your personal statement to do that; write an addendum instead. (Turn to Chapter 6 for a longer discussion of addenda.)

Writing the Essay

Once you've picked a topic and sit down to write, follow these writing tips to give your essay the most impact:

Tip #1: Start with a Bang   All good writing—whether it's a magazine article or a law school application essay—must hook the reader in the first paragraph, preferably in the first sentence. This is where you win or lose your reader. Do not assume that you can win your reader's interest further down in the essay—I often never got that far. On the other hand, if someone caught my attention from the get-go, my interest was his to lose. Opening lines I remember well include, "My marriage nearly ended over dirty dishes," and, "My sister is beautiful, unlike me." Wouldn't you be curious to find out what comes next? "Tattoo Tom," "Morris 405," and "Coast Guard" in Appendix B do an especially good job of hooking the reader in the first paragraph. ("Pretty Horses" has a wonderful ending—also a good thing.)

Tip #2: Keep Your Message Upbeat You might have an interesting story to tell about dealing with adversity, whether it's depression or abuse or a stutter. Make sure that your ultimate message is a positive one, though. It's too easy to feel depressed reading entire essays about someone's fear of loneliness or that dark summer when an applicant was considering suicide. Make sure that the overall image you leave readers with is one of perseverance, determination, and optimism, and provide concrete examples of how you've faced your challenges. Take a look at the hardship described in the "Korea" essay ("I wasn't like the other children at school in Kansas, and they never let me forget it.") and compare it to the difficult circumstances described in "Morris 405." The first essay sounds whiny while the second inspires us. (By the way, a light touch of humor can't hurt, either, with these kinds of topics. If *Leaving Las Vegas* could work in some levity, so can you.)

And don't be stridently negative about a particular viewpoint or people who don't share your beliefs. You don't know the preferences of the person reading your essay. Better to say you're a staunch Democrat than that you hate Republicans. Better to talk about how much you love your book club than how much you detest college athletics.

Tip #3: Don't Start Your Essay with a Famous Quotation It might be the perfect way to express how you feel or introduce the topic of your essay, but not only does opening with a famous quotation violate Tip #1, it's also considered a lazy writing technique. Tell your story in your own words. If you really want to incorporate the quotation into your essay, do so at the very end. The "Jorge" essay uses and abuses quotations like nobody's business—they add nothing to his essay and he gets one of the sources wrong to boot!

On the other hand, if the quotation involves words that really made you think (for an "inflection point" essay, using Technique #3), that might be just the opening bang that your essay needs: "'You smile too much,' my uncle once told me," or, "'You're like a creaky workhorse that just keeps plowing ahead,' my math teacher told me, as a compliment." Typically, quotations from nonfamous people, people who actually spoke directly to you, resonate more strongly than quotations from famous people that you're using just because they capture a sentiment in words better than you can.

TOP TEN MOST OVERUSED SOURCES FOR QUOTATIONS

1. Mark Twain
2. Clarence Darrow
3. Any of the Founding Fathers
4. Any U.S. president
5. Maya Angelou
6. Robert Frost
7. Oliver Wendell Holmes
8. *The Tao of Pooh*
9. Marian Wright Edelman
10. William Shakespeare

Tip #4: Make It Visual   Your essay has to be memorable enough that an admissions officer can recall what you wrote about in a committee meeting a week or two months later. You have to tell a story that she can picture in her mind. Dialogue and sensory descriptions (dialect, smell, feel) are good techniques to help readers visualize your story, but vivid images also do the trick. "Tattoo Tom," "Morris 405," and "Pretty Horses" are all very sensory—the stale smell of the mental ward, the skin covered in tattoos, the erratic clashes of dishes, the strong Brazilian coffees, and the irritating accordion music. "Tattoo Tom" also uses dialogue very effectively.

Tip #5: Skip Artificial Endings   If your essay is truly personal, it sounds awfully strained when you slap on a concluding paragraph talking about why you want to go to School X. The vast majority of personal statements I've read concluded this way, and that kind of ending was always transparent. I knew that applicants simply substituted the school name in every essay, and, to make matters even worse, lots of people mixed up their essays and told me how badly they wanted to go to Columbia or Cornell. If law schools ask for a personal statement, they don't expect you to make token reference to their programs. If you really want to talk about why that law school appeals to you, do so in a full-length statement of purpose, not in a personal statement.

Tip #6: Don't Be Stuck in High School   It's perfectly appropriate to write about events and experiences going back to your childhood or adolescence, but make sure that by the end of your essay you've circled back to the present. For example, don't start your essay with, "I remember fondly the best days of my life, when I was in high school, hanging out with my buddies at the mall, singing along to the crazy lyrics of 'One Week' by the Barenaked Ladies." Or look at the "Jorge" essay: "I can still remember when my weekly allowance was the be-all, end-all of my existence. I would spend the week hatching schemes and plans about how to spend my Friday windfall." Admissions officers look to your essay to get a sense of your maturity (law school will test it in many ways), and they get nervous if an applicant seems stuck in a less-mature stage of his life (that guy we all know who peaked in high school). For example, if you're discussing the values you had in high school, it's fine to mention your fixation on the right clothes and cars and status symbols, but make sure you work in that your outlook has changed, and if it hasn't, pick another topic. Edit any language that sounds immature or generational ("Your clinical program is so amazing."), tone down any hyperbole ("I couldn't believe that they would get rich on the backs of their employees."), and avoid exclamation points ("I told them I had a constitutional right to print whatever I wanted in my school newspaper!"). And make sure to keep things in perspective. In one essay that really struck me as odd, the applicant complained about oppressively high ATM fees after earlier mentioning the snazzy car she had driven in high school. When in doubt, have someone older read your essay for a reality check.

THE STATEMENT OF PURPOSE

Writing a statement of purpose is a much more straightforward process than writing a personal statement, because you have the luxury of answering a specific question rather than having to choose from a million possible personal topics. "Straightforward" doesn't mean easier, however. This essay is easy to write only if you've done a lot of research before making the decision to go to law school. Most people who apply to law school right out of college do so by default and have a really hard time intelligently discussing their motivations for two pages. If you're already out of school and are switching careers, you'll be held to an even higher standard. So even if you haven't done your research before deciding to apply, you need to do it now so that you don't sound clueless.

This essay must present a tight argument. If your motive for pursuing a law degree is to become an environmental lawyer, what in your background makes that a logical next step? Admissions officers will take you much more seriously if you map out the trajectory leading up to that career choice. For example, you may have become interested in bottom-fishing regulations while working on a fishing boat and went off to get a public policy degree with an emphasis on water use. It would make perfect sense for you to decide that you want to become an environmental lawyer. Or take a look at the "Health Law" and "Coast Guard" essays in Appendix B, both of which offer compelling and credible arguments for pursuing a law degree. They are both backward looking (What about my background got me to this point?) and forward looking (What do I hope to accomplish with my law degree?). They both made me conclude: "He knows where he's headed and how he's going to get there. He's mapped out a trajectory for his career, and he has intelligent reasons for pursuing a law degree at this time in his life."

Note that admissions officers know—and hope!—that you'll zigzag throughout law school and beyond as you discover exciting new niches and fields, so you don't have to commit to a narrow career niche, but you should show that you've at least thought about the direction in which you're heading. For example, the "Health Law" author explains, "I might serve as a patent prosecutor or a patent litigator, or as a liaison with regulatory bodies like the FDA." The "Coast Guard" essay gives us a good sense of the legal issues the author needs to be equipped to handle as a Coast Guard attorney: "from search and seizure to international jurisdiction, from criminal law to immigration law." As a bonus, both authors also succeed at conveying their passion for their chosen work, the cutting-edge discoveries in medical research and the dangerous and important missions conducted by the Coast Guard, respectively. As readers, we have no trouble deducing that they will bring that same passion to their legal careers.

Here are some examples of other backgrounds that make sense when you're explaining a career transition into law:

- A science degree for environmental law

- A music or literary background for entertainment or publishing law

- Technology experience or a computer science degree for intellectual property law

- A human resources background for employment law

- Social-work experience for family, elder, or juvenile law

- A tax or finance background for corporate, transactional, or estate-planning law

In these statements of purpose, most people discuss their *interest* in law, but you can also discuss the skills and personality traits that make you well suited for a legal career. This is a good strategy if your background doesn't easily suggest that law is a logical next step but you believe that your personality and larger skill set make law a good match. You'll have to back up your claims with examples and anecdotes from your academic and work experience. You should also make clear that you enjoy using those skills. Examples include:

- Analytical skills

- Research skills

- Writing skills

- Attention to detail

- Time-management skills

Because you haven't been a lawyer yet, you'll need some authority for the premise that these are good skills for lawyers to have—don't expect anyone to assume that you know what you're talking about. To give your argument authority, you can refer to your conversations with the lawyers and law students you interviewed or observed. (See the next page.)

That's how you wow them with a statement of purpose. If you have trouble making a solid, two-page argument for going to law school, you should be rethinking whether law school is the right choice for you. If your gut is telling you that this is the right choice but you're having trouble articulating your motives, I have a homework assignment for you. Here's a checklist of research you should do before you sit down to write your statement of purpose.

Wowing Them with Research

Research Tip #1: Classes If you have an opportunity to take law-related classes, sign up for them. College-level law classes (usually some variation on Constitutional Law) have very little to do with real law school classes and even less to do with the practice of law, but at a minimum these kinds of classes will allow you to make a straight-faced argument that they whetted your appetite and got you thinking seriously of law as a career. Be forewarned, though: You'll have to ace these classes. You might get away with arguing that you flubbed your chemistry class because it's not your forte, but admissions officers won't cut you any slack for underperforming in pre-law classes. Auditing these classes is an option, but not one I recommend. If you're serious about going to law school, you should be taking the class seriously enough to earn a grade.

Research Tip #2: Lawyers   Talk to lawyers, as many as you can find. Ask your friends and family for references, and ask those references for even more names. Find law school students and lawyers who went to your college (you can find them on www.martindale.com, a database of practicing lawyers, and through your school's alumni office). Interview as many as you can and ask for referrals. Here are the kinds of questions to ask them:

- What kind of law do they practice?

- Where did they go to law school?

- What classes were the most useful?

- What do they like about practicing law?

- What skills do they find most important?

- If they had to do it over again, what would they do differently?

Then repeat this drill with law students. The more informed you sound about your career choice, the more compelling your essay argument will be. The "Health Law" essay makes very clear, for example, that the author spoke to real lawyers, because most nonlawyers haven't heard of the distinction between a patent prosecutor and a patent litigator.

Another benefit of this kind of research is that you'll start law school with a solid network already in place. Networks come in handy when you're looking for a job or plain old career advice.

A side note: For your own purposes, it could be helpful to speak with people who attended law school but decided not to practice, as well as people who practiced for a while but left the law. What benefit did they get from their law degrees? Was the training still useful? Could they have ended up where they are now without their law degrees? Would a different degree have been more useful? Those are all good conversations to have, but don't highlight those in your essay. The consensus among most admissions officers is that if you don't plan on practicing law or working with the law in some fashion (say, as a legislator or a law professor), you shouldn't be going to law school. And they are right.

Research Tip #3: Career Counseling   Take advantage of all career counseling options available to you. If you're still in school, go to your career center and read every book and magazine and survey you can find. Take career assessment and personality tests to demonstrate that you're taking this juncture in your life seriously. Many schools offer career counseling services to their alums as well. If that's not an option for you, you'll find plenty of books and websites on the subject. Bear one caveat in mind, however. In my experience, there are some truly great career counselors out there and some god-awful ones, both on campus and off. Don't take everything they say as gospel truth, and if you're not confident in the career counselors available to you, keep looking. At a minimum, a good career counselor should have real-world work experience outside of academia. If not, look for other counsel to supplement their insights.

Research Tip #4: Legal Work   Take a job in a law office or legal aid clinic, even if it's just for a couple of hours a week. There's nothing like experiencing the nasty underbelly of legal practice to find out what that life is really like, and the more exposure you have to real-life lawyering—as opposed to TV shows and movies and paperbacks—the better. As with pre-law classes, law schools don't really care whether you have legal experience before applying, but being able to refer to it in your statement of purpose will give you authority; it shows not just that you know what you're getting into but also that you cared enough to find out. You can also use this opportunity to interview lawyers and develop your network.

Research Tip #5: In-house Lawyers   If you're out of school and work in a nonlegal capacity, track down the in-house lawyers at your company or, if there are none, find the people in your company who deal with legal matters and outside lawyers. Every business has to deal with a headache-inducing number of legal rules and regulations, whether they relate to employment, tax, contracts, pensions, patents, or work-safety matters. Find out what kinds of issues those colleagues deal with, what kinds of lawyers they work with, and what it takes to do that kind of in-house legal work.

Bad Reasons

Here are examples of reasons you *shouldn't* give for wanting a law degree (even if they are the god's honest truth):

Bad Reason #1: The Economy Do not give the impression that you're applying to law school because you're terrified of throwing yourself into a dismal job market. I would guess that *most* people applying to law school in down cycles do so for this reason, but you'll look like a loser if you can't give better reasons than that. You'll also look unconfident and unprepared.

A special note for PhD students: Unless you're applying to a very academic law school like Yale or Chicago, if you're leaving a PhD program before you're done, or applying as you finish a PhD, you'll have to make clear that that's not the only reason you're applying to law school. Even if a law school does not ask for a statement of purpose, you should submit one to dispel any worries that you're just moving on to the next degree. The less marketable your PhD is, the more important this task is—chemistry PhDs don't really need to explain their motives as much as English PhDs do.

And a special note for the unemployed: If you've been out of school for a while and you're in a field with a lot of layoffs, such as technology or manufacturing, explain why this *isn't* the only reason you're going to law school. It can be part of the reason: "I always wanted to go, but this job paid the bills and I couldn't justify quitting and going into debt for school. Here's my chance." You don't need to write more on that issue—the rest of the essay should be about why you want to do this, what your old career brings to the table, and what your plans are.

Bad Reason #2: Kindergarten Dreams Maybe you really have wanted to be a lawyer since you were five years old, but who cares? Why would anyone trust the career instincts of a five-year-old? A shocking number of applicants offer this reason for applying, and it never stops sounding inane. And don't tell us that your parents or your junior high school social studies teacher or whoever said you should be a lawyer because you "love to talk and argue."

Bad Reason #3: Courtroom Drama One of the first classes you'll take in law school is Civil Procedure. Count your blessings that you can't recite those rules from memory yet. What you'll find out soon enough is that most legal disputes get resolved long before they ever get to a jury because of those Civil Procedure rules, and many lawyers have only ever seen juries on TV. If you're looking for theatrics and public speaking, admissions officers will wonder why you want a job that typically involves long hours writing briefs or contracts all by your lonesome self. If you've done your research properly, you'll already have disabused yourself of this misconception.

Bad Reason #4: Buying Time   Many applicants have no idea what career they want to pursue, and they want a law degree as an all-purpose degree. There's some truth to the all-purpose reputation of the JD, but over the past few decades that reputation has become less deserved. Most lawyers have to specialize early on in their careers to stay ahead of the competition, and while some lawyers will always jump over the fence to pursue new careers outside of law, many of them find that they didn't really need law degrees to get there. You want to give the impression that you're in charge of your career, not that you're following the herd, waiting to see where a law degree will take you.

Bad Reason #5: Lineage   Lawyers tend to breed more lawyers, so many applicants write about law as the family business. It's not a bad thing to be following family tradition, but it's not a very good argument for why you want to go to law school. You'll improve the forcefulness of your argument if you can demonstrate that you've explored other career options with some seriousness but still chose law for intelligent reasons.

Bad Reason #6: Hollywood   So your favorite movie is *Legally Blonde*. Who doesn't have a few guilty pleasures? Save those for the TiVo, though. You'll sound silly if you make any reference to fake lawyers. Admissions officers aren't unaware of the strong cultural influence—when I was an attorney interviewing law school students, I watched their hemlines rise dramatically during the height of *Ally McBeal*—but they won't take you very seriously if you based your most important career decision on a movie or a TV show, especially one created by David E. Kelley. The same goes for any book by John Grisham.

Bad Reason #7: Desperation   If you're switching careers, be careful not to give the impression that you're fleeing your existing line of work. You want to persuade admissions officers that you have positive and well-informed reasons for making this career change. I interviewed quite a few engineers, for example, who told me how much they hated designing those eight-sided thingies, that they were just bored to death and couldn't wait to become patent attorneys. I was never quite sure if they believed me when I explained that as patent attorneys, their job would be to *describe* those eight-sided thingies in anesthetizing detail for the bureaucrats at the U.S. Patent and Trademark Office. So make clear in your essay that you understand what you're getting yourself into. If you hate your job because you're a glorified secretary and you feel as if your education is going to waste, keep all such thoughts to yourself; most young attorneys feel that way, too. You don't want people to think, "Wow, this person is really going to hate being a lawyer."

Researching Schools

Some law schools ask you to address not only why you want a law degree, but also why you want it from their school in particular. Don't even bother with generic references to reputation, class size, or commitment to teaching—that won't fool anyone. You'll need to do another round of research to prove to admissions officers that you've done your homework and that you have good reasons for choosing that particular law school. Because the *U.S. News* rankings penalize law schools for every offer they make that an applicant turns down, admissions officers prefer to admit people who are likely to accept their offers. Here are some ways you can persuade them of your sincerity:

Research Tip #1: Students and Alums   Talk to current students and alums of that law school. What did they like about the law school? Were there particular experiences or professors that made their time there worthwhile? Why did they choose that school? Are they happy with their decision? You'll find them more likely and eager to talk to you if they know you through some mutual acquaintance or if they went to your college. Unless they're speaking to you confidentially, you can and should mention them by name in your essay. (Admissions officers will be grateful to them for being such good ambassadors.)

Research Tip #2: Admissions Reps   As an admissions officer, I traveled all around the country speaking to potential applicants at colleges and law school forums sponsored by the LSAC, and I sent alums and current students to events I couldn't make. Those recruiting events are excellent opportunities to ask law school reps what they think makes their schools special. In the fall, you should be able to find each law school's recruiting schedule on its website, and you can find law school forum dates at www.lsac.org. Before you talk to any law school reps, though, read Chapter 7 on interviewing. I always took notes at those events: a star next to the names of candidates I wanted to recruit more heavily and an X next to the names of candidates whose files would go straight into the "denied" pile. Even though these meetings aren't formal interviews, you should treat them as if they were. In your application you'll want to mention the reps you meet by name, so be sure to get their business cards.

Research Tip #3: Law School Websites You'll find a lot of useful information on law schools' websites. Say you're interested in intellectual property law. You can probably find out that Professor Turbonerd teaches a seminar on copyright litigation and recently published an article on property rights in cyberspace, that the IP Law Association recently sponsored a debate on music downloading, that the school's IP law clinic is working on a trademark infringement case you've been tracking, and that you have the opportunity to pursue a joint JD and master's degree in computer science.

Finally, note that you can mention any legitimate reason you have for wanting to go to that law school, even if it's not career-related, like a family commitment. It's perfectly appropriate, for example, to explain that you need to be near St. Louis because your wife will be starting a medical residency there.

THE DIVERSITY ESSAY

Some schools also invite you to submit an optional diversity essay ("How would you add to the diversity of the class?" or something along those lines). If you're part of a demographic group that's underrepresented in higher education or you have an unusual background, by all means write about that. (If you're already submitting a personal statement about your interesting background, you can treat the diversity essay as an opportunity to discuss something else that you'll add to the incoming class.)

Please, please don't apologize for being white, male, and middle-class—every white middle-class guy does that. And don't joke about how it's obvious that they're looking to admit lots of poor people and minorities, so the fact that you're white, male, and rich makes you diverse. You can find *something* about your life, work, or school experience that will set you apart from most of your law school classmates. Maybe you have an engineering degree, were raised by Christian Scientists, speak three languages, or started your own business. This essay can be shorter than your primary essay, so you shouldn't have to strain too much to write something interesting; three full paragraphs are fine. If you have a lot to say, you can make it a full-length essay, if the particular application permits.

When writing your diversity essay, pay special attention to the "keep your message upbeat" rule. If you've ever suffered hardship or hurt feelings because of a trait that makes you different or a goal that you've pursued, it's okay to discuss those downsides—your essay has to be credible, after all—but don't try any cheap ploys for sympathy, and don't whine. You have to be a tough cookie to get through law school and an even tougher cookie to practice law, and you don't want an admissions officer to question your ability to make it.

FINAL TIPS

Whether you're submitting a personal statement, a statement of purpose, or a diversity essay, make sure to follow these rules:

Rule #1: Edit and Proofread, Then Proofread Again
Your grammar, spelling, and punctuation must be flawless. When in doubt, pull out those old standbys *The Chicago Manual of Style* and Strunk & White. If grammar, spelling, and punctuation aren't your strong points, enlist a friend to help (and give you a tutorial, while you're at it). There's no excuse for a college graduate to mess this up. And beware the spell-check trap—it won't catch "right" when you should have written "write," and it won't catch your "commitment to pubic service." (You laugh, but I saw that typo as a law review editor.) Always have a second pair of eyes proofread your essays before you send them off.

RESOURCES FOR THE GRAMMATICALLY AND RHETORICALLY CHALLENGED

The Chicago Manual of Style
Strunk & White, *The Elements of Style*
Patricia T. O'Conner, *Words Fail Me*
Mitchell Ivers, *Random House Guide to Good Writing*
Constance Hale, *Sin and Syntax*

Rule #2: Nothing Cutesy Anything cutesy or gimmicky will make admissions officers groan. Stay away from the following:

- Essays in the form of poetry

- Essays in the form of a legal brief ("For all the reasons cited above, the admissions committee should admit Petitioner to Slamdunk Law School.")

- Essays in the form of an obituary ("Tracy Johnson died the most respected jurist of her time.")

- Essays in the form of an interview

- Crayons, construction paper, perfume, or illustrated essays, no matter how sophisticated

Rule #3: No Legalisms You're not a lawyer yet, so your use of legal concepts or terminology will most likely demonstrate that you have no idea what you're talking about, not to mention the fact that legal writing is considered god-awful by the rest of the world, including admissions officers. Many applicants, for example, refer to a company or a person violating someone's right to free speech, when, in fact, the First Amendment applies only to *government* restrictions on speech. And by all means, steer clear of anything in Latin.

Rule #4: Show, Don't Tell   Back up any general statements with examples and anecdotes. If you write, "The student presidency taught me that leadership means more than delegating," tell us *how* you learned that lesson. What were the conflicts and problems you faced? If you write, "I have excellent time-management skills," back up that statement by pointing out that you graduated in the top 10 percent of an engineering program that 40 percent of engineering freshmen drop.

Rule #5: Respect Page Limits and Other Minutiae   If a school gives you a page or word limit, abide by it. And follow the spirit of the rule as well as the letter—don't get too sneaky with fonts, margins, and line spacing. Admissions officers won't cut you any slack if your essay comes in under the page limit but makes them go cross-eyed because the font or line spacing is so small. If a school doesn't specify a length, a good rule of thumb is two to three pages, double-spaced, in eleven-point Times New Roman, with one-inch margins all around. When in doubt, shorter is better than longer. As an admissions officer buddy of mine likes to say: "The vast, vast, vast majority of just-out-of-college applicants (almost all applicants, really) are not interesting enough to fill six pages. Show me that you understand my time is valuable, and show me that you understand how to pick out what's really important."

Make sure to put your name and Social Security number in a header and page numbers in a footer, just in case your file goes splat and has to be reassembled. Also, identify in the header what essay question you're answering, if you're given more than one option or are submitting more than one essay ("Personal Statement," "Optional Essay #3," etc.). By the way, you don't need to give your essay a title like "Morris 405" or "Jorge." I added those titles in the appendix essays so that I could refer to them easily in this chapter.

Don't submit pages that are crumpled, stained, or smell like pot smoke—most admissions officers really aren't looking for that contact high. Really, your essay shouldn't smell like any kind of smoke.

And finally, if you're getting too close to your material and think you're losing perspective, turn to the sample essays in the appendix to keep your big-picture objective in mind. Can you see how much more engaging and revealing the good ones are?

CHAPTER 4

Damning with Faint Praise:
Recommendations

I once reviewed a recommendation written by a Nobel Prize–winning professor. Here's what it said, in full: "Matthew was a student in my Principles of Microeconomics lecture class. He received a B+. I'm sure he will be a fine addition to your law school class." What else could he say? Good old Matthew was probably a nameless, faceless blob wedged among two hundred students in an auditorium-sized classroom, and it's likely he interacted exclusively with his graduate student TA. To be fair, that professor shouldn't have agreed to write a recommendation for someone he didn't really know (*he* should have known better), but Matthew could have been smarter and savvier about the recommendation process.

Not all recommendations are that useless, but many of them come close. The sad truth is that the vast majority of recommendations make no real difference in the application process, because they are complimentary but too generic and bland to convey anything meaningful about the applicant or anything that makes him or her stand out in any way. They just aren't memorable. On the flip side, I have admitted applicants who would otherwise have ended up in the so-called ding pile (rejection pile) solely as a result of a bang-up, standout recommendation. They were few and far between, but a great recommendation can make that big a difference.

There's only so much control you have over your recommendations as an applicant, but there are things you can do to avoid some very common mistakes and to maximize the chances that your recommendations will stand out—in a good way.

LOGISTICS

It's boring to start with logistics, but these are the kinds of questions I always get first, and the logistics can determine whom you ask for your letters.

Logistics Tip #1: How to Submit? Law schools don't want to receive recommendations directly from you, unless you are merely forwarding an envelope sealed and signed (over the flap) by your recommender. That leaves you a couple of options: (1) You can have your recommenders submit the letters directly to your law schools; (2) your college might offer a service whereby it collects your recommendations from your professors and then forwards them to your law schools; or (3) you can use a service offered by the Law School Admission Council (LSAC) called the LSDAS (Law School Data Assembly Service). I strongly encourage you to use the LSDAS recommendation service, unless a law school you're applying to tells you not to.

The LSDAS service offers two big advantages over the old-fashioned snail-mail method:

▪ Your recommenders have to write only one letter that they send to LSAC, and then LSAC distributes it to all of your law schools. With the snail-mail method, your recommenders have to mail a separate copy to each school, which means you and your recommenders have to keep track of different addresses, different envelopes, etc., and make sure the letters don't go to the wrong schools.

▪ You can go to your account at www.lsac.org to look up the status of your recommendations: what letters have been submitted, and when they were sent off to your law schools. Using the snail-mail method, you have to keep calling your recommenders and your law schools to find out who has received what and when, a huge source of anxiety for applicants.

LSAC now lets you indicate online which letters you want sent to which schools, and you should be careful when dealing with school-specific letters. For example, if you're having a UVA law school alum write a letter about how perfect you would be for UVA, you don't want that letter sent to any other school. LSAC does not screen the recommendation letters it receives, so don't expect someone on that end to catch school-specific letters.

As a practical matter, if the UVA alum would still make a great recommender for the other law schools, you should also have that person write a regular recommendation letter that *can* be sent to all your schools.

Keep in mind as you manage your deadlines that LSAC needs to receive your recommendations at least two weeks before you want your law schools to receive them.

Logistics Tip #2: How Many?   Most schools ask for one or two recommendations, but ultimately you should make sure to follow their specific directions. If a school asks for two, for example, you should have a very good reason to submit more than two, even if a school tells you that you won't be penalized for submitting more than the required number. Admissions officers dread the files that land on their desks with a thud.

Also note that if you use the LSDAS recommendation service, your recommenders will be using the generic LSDAS recommendation form, which most likely deviates to some degree from the specific questions listed on an individual law school's recommendation form. As long as a law school tells you it's okay to use the LSDAS form, your recommenders can go ahead and use it. However, it's in your interest to see what qualities those law schools ask about on their own forms and make sure that your recommenders still cover those qualities, even though the LSDAS form doesn't specifically ask about them. (See page 111.)

Logistics Tip #3: Dean's Certifications Some law schools ask for a Dean's Certification, which is a form to be filled out by administrative officials at your college. The Certification does not count toward the number of recommendation letters a law school requires. The person who fills out the Certification does not need to know you personally. Your school officials are usually asked to do things like the following in that letter:

- Certify that you are (or were, if you've already graduated) in good standing at your college.

- Discuss any disciplinary actions or proceedings involving you.

- List your actual or estimated class rank.

- List your major.

- List your GPA.

- List any honors you received.

Your college will have its own procedures about who will fill out the form. It's usually the dean of students, the registrar, or the pre-law adviser. The LSDAS does not process Dean's Certifications, so you will have to use each law school's specific Certification form, and your schools will have to send them to the individual law schools.

Logistics Tip #4: Waivers   Under federal law (the Buckley Amendment), you have the right to inspect any letters of recommendation contained in your applicant file at the law school you ultimately attend, unless you expressly waive that right. That law also prohibits schools from requiring you to waive those inspection rights, so law school recommendation forms all make you declare, by checking a box at the top of the recommendation form, whether or not you waive those rights. You have to fill that part out before you give the form to your recommenders, so that they know whether you will have access to that letter when you get to law school.

So should you waive those rights? Personally, as an admissions officer, I didn't care if applicants did or didn't, because I believed (and still do) that recommenders should have the courage to state their true opinion to your face, or at least politely decline if they don't have good things to say about you. Not all admissions officers feel that way, though, and certainly not all recommenders will feel comfortable without a waiver.

One concern I hear all the time from applicants is that if they check the waiver box, their recommenders can't show them their letters even if they want to. Waiving your rights under that federal law does *not* prohibit you from seeing drafts or final copies of your recommendation letters if your recommenders want to share them with you. What you are waiving is your right to go to officials at the law school you end up attending and to demand to see copies of your recommendations in their files. So checking the waiver box

doesn't stand in the way of collaborating with your recommenders in the letter-writing process, nor does it prohibit
your recommenders from showing you copies as a courtesy
or for future use.

Do your recommenders care whether you can see the
recommendation? I can't answer that for you. Some do and
some don't. I would have that conversation with your recommenders—explain what the waiver means, and explain
that you want to check the box for the benefit of admissions
officers, but that it doesn't preclude you from seeing drafts of
the recommendation *if the recommender would find that
helpful.* I emphasize that last bit because it's a nice way to
signal to recommenders that you would be happy to collab-
orate without being pushy about it. They can decide for
themselves whether they want to show you their letters.
Whether or not they involve you in the process, you should
go ahead and check the box so that admissions officers know
you can't demand the letters from them against the potential wishes of the recommender.

Logistics Tip #5: Gratitude   Once you know your recommendation letters have arrived at LSAC, break out the
good stationery and send your recommenders heartfelt
thank-you notes. If you've done this right, and they've done
this right, your recommenders will have given considerable
thought and time to this exercise, and they will appreciate
your thanks. A bottle of wine or a box of Godiva chocolates
wouldn't be unwelcome or inappropriate, either. And when

you've accepted an offer and know where you'll be headed the coming fall, let them know the good news.

HOW TO PICK YOUR RECOMMENDERS

Avoid jumping all over the first person who offers to write you a "great recommendation." Recommendation writing is both an art and a science, and few people do it really well, either because they don't know you well enough to address the things admissions officers care about, because they can't be bothered, or because they don't know how.

Recommender Tip #1: Academic Recommenders   Many law schools state an express preference for academic recommendations, meaning someone who has taught you in college and can speak to your strengths as a student and a scholar. The reason they do that is because they look to your recommendations to try to predict, as best they can, how you'll do in law school, so they want to get a sense of your talents in the classroom. If the LSAT score is meant to give them an idea of your intellectual horsepower, your recommendations (along with your transcript) are supposed to let them gauge what you do with that horsepower. We all know people who are whip sharp but slackers in the classroom, and people who have to work their buns off to perform well—admissions officers want to figure out where you fall on that continuum.

If you've been out of college for more than two years, admissions officers understand that it can be very difficult to track down your old college professors, and they'll cut you some slack. If you're in a graduate program, you can ask one of your graduate professors to write a letter. If you're out in the working world, you can ask your boss. If an undergraduate recommendation is at all possible, though, you should try to drum one up, and submit a second, nonacademic one (if required) from one of these alternate sources.

Of your various professors, the most useful ones are going to be those who taught classes that approximate law school the best: classes that are heavy on analytical reasoning, reading, research, and expository writing. Recommendations from classes like Theater, Communications, Creative Writing, Statistics, and Conversational French won't be as useful.

Recommenders that are almost always useless for the purposes of law school admissions include your state senator, friends of the family, relatives, famous people and muckety-muck judges who know you only socially (if at all), your lacrosse coach, and your choir director.

If you're still in school or a recent graduate, and you have some experience working in a legal capacity (as a paralegal, say, or an intern at a legal clinic), you can certainly submit a recommendation from the people you've worked for. Just make sure they are supplemental recommendation letters rather than substitutes for your academic recommendations.

If a school states no preference for the type of recommender they're looking for, assume they prefer an academic one. And if any school gives you instructions that contradict what I'm telling you here, follow those instructions.

Recommender Tip #2: Closeness Trumps Rank Remember poor old Matthew from the beginning of the chapter? He made a classic mistake: He assumed that a recommendation from a Nobel Prize winner was too good an opportunity to pass up, and he didn't stop to ask himself what that professor would be able to say about him. Matthew would have been much better off asking his TA for that class to write his recommendation (or picking another class entirely for his recommendation). His TA would have been able to base his recommendation on their weekly discussion groups and weekly assignments that the TA graded. Many law school applicants attend colleges that do not enable up-close-and-personal relationships with professors—some people spend four years interacting only with graduate students—and they shouldn't worry that they are at a disadvantage with respect to their recommendations. The person writing the recommendation should be able to speak with experience and authority about you in the classroom, and if that means you have to forgo the Nobel Prize winner, that's okay—you're better off with the TA. The same principle applies if your recommendation is coming from the working world. You're better off requesting a letter from the congressional staffer you worked with and reported to every day than the bigwig senator who still mispronounces your name or confuses you with the aide who worked for him three sessions ago.

Once you've cleared that hurdle, if you're choosing between someone with less teaching experience and someone with more, pick the latter. Being able to speak from the experience of teaching ten years' or fifteen years' or even decades' worth of undergraduates will give a teacher's opinion more weight. A TA won't have been teaching that long, and calling you the best student he's ever taught won't sound impressive if this is his first year teaching.

A caveat: While it's generally true that law schools prefer academic recommendations over professional ones, there's a tipping point for older applicants where it starts to look funny if you *don't* provide a recommendation from your employer. Unless you've been out of college for at least seven or ten years, though, or unless a school specifically prefers or requires a professional recommendation, you're still better off trying to drum up at least one academic one if you can.

Recommender Tip #3: Seminars Trump Lectures   Why? Because your professors get to know you in seminars in a way they can't in lecture classes. The more class participation opportunities you have, and the more substantial the writing and research you do for a class, the better able your professor will be to discuss your academic talents. If you're reading this book in your undergraduate years, try to take multiple seminars with a professor with whom you really hit it off. Even better, take on a major project with a professor, like a thesis.

Seminars tend to be higher-level classes, so you probably won't be able to take them until your junior year, at the earliest. Your professor will need at least the entire semester, if not multiple semesters, to get to know you and your work, so plan ahead. You'll need time to cultivate those relationships.

Recommender Tip #4: Willing and Able It's human nature: People are busy at best, lazy at worst, and don't like writing bang-up recommendations except for the few pet students and employees they really want to go to bat for. And that's under the best of circumstances. With the huge upsurge in law school applications in recent years, professors and bosses are bombarded with recommendation requests, and they grant many that they shouldn't. Why? Because they are usually nice people who don't have the heart to say no, even though they don't have the time or the energy or the knowledge to write meaningful letters, letters that will really help your cause with admissions officers. So be smart about how you approach people. You should ask professors to be candid with you:

- Do they have time to write a recommendation for you? Tell them you understand that they are deluged with requests and that a well-crafted and effective recommendation letter takes time and effort. Ask them politely to decline if they don't think they can make that commitment right now. This also gives them an easy out if they don't think they can write you a favorable letter.

- Do they think they can write a very strong letter on your behalf? If they say no, be gracious and thank them for their honesty. Make clear that you're happy to approach someone else if they have any reservations at all, and explain that you'd still love to hear their constructive feedback for your own benefit.

If there is any resistance or push-back or wavering, anything less than an enthusiastic commitment right off the bat, let it go. Thank them and move on. There will be times when you have taken a number of classes with a professor or worked very closely with a boss who has gotten to know you very well, but you suspect that she is not one of your greatest fans for one reason or another. Maybe she doesn't like your writing style. Maybe he doesn't like your view of Plato, or how you handled the Crisco account. Maybe she's sick of losing her top people to law school. Maybe you'll lose your bonus if he gets wind that you'll be bailing. Whatever the reason, you're better off finding someone else. Closeness and status don't help if a recommender isn't going to say great things about you.

Recommender Tip #5: Collaboration   Also try to gauge whether your potential recommenders would be willing to work with you on the letter. They should be grateful to receive that offer of help—and many will be—but some won't be open to collaboration at all. All else being equal, pick the person who is willing to work with you and understand why you're applying to law school, what you're trying to communicate in your applications, and how you're trying to present yourself.

For example, I recall reading an application essay that set forth all the compelling reasons why that particular applicant wanted to leverage his banking and finance experience as a corporate lawyer. You can imagine my eyebrow cocking when I got to the recommendation letter written by his boss at the bank, who explained that the applicant wanted to go to law school so he could be an "agent for social change." Those things aren't inherently exclusive of each other, but the recommendation just wasn't in sync with the rest of the application, which hadn't talked at all about wanting to bring about social change. It felt like something the recommender had just thrown in there because he thought that must be what law schools want to hear.

How do you make sure that your messages are in sync? By being prepared and giving them the information they need to write their letters. Collect the information that you want your recommenders to have:

▨ A letter explaining

- why you're applying to law school;
- what schools you're applying to (your list doesn't have to be final, but if, for example, you're applying only to New York or D.C. schools, your recommenders should know that, and why);
- how you're positioning yourself in the rest of your application (if you're far enough along with your drafts, you should include your personal statement or statement of purpose; good recommenders will demand them);
- which qualities you want them to address in their letters (you'll compile that list from the individual law schools' recommendation forms), along with suggested anecdotes and examples to illustrate them; and

- when the letters are due (i.e., when *you* want them submitted to LSDAS), and when you'll be checking in with them to follow up

■ Your résumé

■ Your transcript

■ Copies of any graded class work and assignments for that professor, as well as any exams you've taken for that class; for a professional recommender, copies of any reports, assignments, memos, and evaluations

■ Stamped and addressed envelopes for mailing the letters to LSAC

It's best to present this information to them when you both have some time to review it together. Offer to take your recommender out to lunch or coffee so you can have a heart-to-heart about your strategy and your goals, and also so you can refresh your recommender's memory about your talents and performance. Make sure they know how to get in touch with you if they have any follow-up questions or run into any problems.

Explaining your goals is particularly important when you meet with your recommenders, because many professors and employers despair at losing their top talent to law schools. They are not wrong in concluding that law school is a default choice for many college students and employees looking for a career change. You will go a long way toward winning their unqualified support if you can persuade them that you've really thought about why you want a law degree and what your long-term career goals are.

Recommender Tip #6: Show-offs Most professors think they are A+, world-class recommendation writers when in fact, as I explained above, most are far from it. If a professor shows off about how great his recommendations are, don't assume it's true. Better to run far away—in my experience, those are the people who are the most clueless about what a good law school recommendation looks like. I'd be especially wary of people who claim to have a great reputation with law school admissions committees or to have some kind of special "in" at the admissions office. There's way too much turnover among admissions officers at law schools to assume that the person who ends up reading your file will have even heard of that professor. The delusions of grandeur are hilarious from the admissions officer's side of the fence, but it's not funny for the applicant.

Recommender Tip #7: Presentation I'm almost embarrassed to have to say this, but I've seen this all too often: Make sure you choose someone who can write well. It's shocking how badly some recommenders write. Sometimes one gets the sense that they're just hasty and sloppy and haven't proofread their work, but other times it's clear that they're just bad writers, plain and simple. Bad writing gravely undermines whatever good things they might have to say about you.

Recommender Tip #8: Timeliness Be wary of professors who are habitually, chronically, congenitally tardy or disorganized. I've seen too many applications held up by recommenders, when the entire file is complete but for that one letter. Some people end up missing the application deadline entirely because of their recommenders. *Don't let this happen to you.* If the best person to write your recommendation has a problem with deadlines, you need to ask early and often and ride him hard, or pick someone else altogether.

WHAT YOUR RECOMMENDERS
SHOULD WRITE

You should find out, before you write your cover letter to your recommenders, exactly what qualities the different law schools you are applying to want your recommenders to address. (That list goes into your cover letter to your recommenders.) Even if you are using the LSDAS recommendation service and the LSDAS recommendation form (rather than the schools' recommendation forms), your recommenders need to address the qualities that the individual law schools care about, and you'll find those in the schools' own forms. The qualities listed on the LSDAS form are not nearly as specific as many schools' forms. Unless you're going to have your recommenders write different letters for each school you apply to (justifiably, most recommenders aren't willing to go that far), they will need to write one global letter that covers all the bases. Here are some typical qualities that law schools ask recommenders to discuss to the extent they can, just to give you some idea:

- Intellect and native intelligence

- Academic performance

- Analytical skills and reasoning ability

- Written communication skills

- Oral communication skills

- Independence of thought and creativity

- Quality of class participation

- Work ethic and self-discipline

- Enthusiasm and dedication

- Character and ethics

- Maturity and common sense

- Leadership qualities

- Potential for the study of law

- Cooperativeness and concern for others

Guidelines for Recommenders

Here are some guidelines that you can share with your recommenders (you might even show them this section), so that the end result shows off your fine qualities as effectively as possible:

Effectiveness Tip #1: Academics First The primary purpose of a recommendation is to give admissions officers a sense of your academic prowess and accomplishments. Everything else is icing. So professors can certainly talk about your great sense of humor and the great work you've done raising money to fight illiteracy, but not at the expense of your academic talents. Take a look at the recommendation for Madeleine in Appendix C: All but the last paragraph deal with her performance in the classroom.

Similarly, if you have to ask an employer or former employer for a recommendation because you are unable, at this stage in your life, to track down enough professors from your college days, try to pick one who can address the skills that law schools will care about the most:

■ Your analytical skills

■ Your writing skills

■ Your speaking skills

■ Your research skills

■ Your persuasive skills

■ Your problem-solving skills

In Sara's recommendation in the appendix, we get the sense that her job was not the most glamorous. That's okay—part-time jobs and internships usually aren't. But her recommender was able to convey Sara's professionalism, her research skills, her motivation, and her language skills, all things that will be relevant in law school and in legal practice. We also know that Sara has seen legal practice up close and can safely conclude that she knows what she's doing in pursuing a law degree.

Your employer should also emphasize any aspects of your job that support your reasons for applying to law school, as well as any exposure you've had to the law. For example:

> Stephanie has been instrumental in helping us structure our contracts to make sure they meet the complex requirements that we must meet under federal law in order to be deemed a minority-owned business for the purposes of our government sales. She has had to familiarize herself with various statutes and regulations, and she interacts on a regular basis, and at very high levels, with our in-house and external attorneys. Stephanie aspires to become general counsel for a Fortune 500 company, and based on what I've seen of her talents, I have no doubt that she will reach that goal.

Effectiveness Tip #2: Fill in the Gaps   One of the reasons you want to discuss your positioning strategy with your recommender is because you want to make sure the different pieces of your recommendation aren't redundant, and also to fill in the gaps when it comes to tooting your horn.

For example, if your essay revolves around your passion for Gilbert and Sullivan musicals, an admissions officer won't know just from your essay or résumé or transcript that you studied Latin and Ancient Greek so that you could do original-language research for your history thesis on the influence of Aristotle on Thomas Aquinas. Your recommendations are a place for your advocates to show off your talents and accomplishments that are difficult to highlight elsewhere in any depth or that appear too show-offy if you dwell on them yourself. Don't be shy in discussing with your recommenders what accomplishments you'd like them to cover—most recommenders appreciate that. For example, in Madeleine's recommendation, it is easier and more credible for the recommender to point out that the poetry readings Madeleine organized "enjoy the largest and most faithful following among the university's extracurricular offerings."

Your recommender can also help you play against type. If the rest of your application suggests that you are a serious and cerebral scholar, your recommender can mention your whimsical sense of humor and your spot-on Neil Diamond impersonation in karaoke contests.

Effectiveness Tip #3: Anecdotes, Not Adjectives If there's one tip that I wish I could share with every recommender, it's this: Rather than simply stating their *opinions* about a candidate, recommenders should present a persuasive *argument* for their opinions, and that requires *evidence* in the form of examples, stories, and anecdotes. (By the way, if recommenders applied the same standards to their own recommendation letters that they apply to their students' papers, most of them would flunk.)

Most recommenders write letters full of adjectives, even superlatives, but they need to back up those adjectives with facts, examples, and anecdotes. Ninety-nine percent of recommendations don't do that, and for that reason they don't help the applicant or the admissions officer. To be helpful, recommendations need to be memorable, and to be memorable, they need to *show*, not tell. It's for this reason that you need to take such care in picking recommenders who really know you, because if they can't back up their opinions with evidence from their interactions with you, their recommendations won't be worth the paper they're written on.

Typical recommendation:

Pamela is intellectually inquisitive in a way that very few undergraduates are, and I have enjoyed her hungry intellect in my classroom. In her assignments, she always pushes herself further than is expected or required.

Effective recommendation:

Pamela is intellectually inquisitive in a way that very few undergraduates are, and I have enjoyed her hungry intellect in my classroom. In her assignments, she always pushes herself further than is expected or required. For example, she recently wrote a ten-page paper for me on the concept of virtue in Montaigne's Essays. It was excellent—one of the finer undergraduate papers of this length I have read. In one of my notes to her in the margins, I mentioned that she herself was proposing a very Aristotelian notion of virtue, whereupon she promptly came to see me in my office and we had an hour-long conversation on these competing concepts in Montaigne and Aristotle. She has since proposed a longer term paper on the subject (perhaps to evolve into a senior thesis), expanding the comparison to include the Christian concept of virtue as expressed in the letters of Saint Paul.

Typical recommendation:

Dave has great presentation skills and an infectious enthusiasm.

Effective recommendation:

Dave has great presentation skills and an infectious enthusiasm. About six months ago, as a training exercise in public speaking, we asked him and his cohorts each to give a ten-minute presentation on the topic of their choice in a room full of about 150 people. We told them that the topics weren't really that important, that the exercise would focus on their presentation skills. Dave chose to talk about how to make the world's best tuna salad. For ten minutes! And he had the crowd in stitches—people are still talking about it. He's a blend of teacher and stand-up comedian that is born, not made. We now have him teaching that public-speaking seminar.

You can also compare the rich details and anecdotes in Madeleine's and Sara's recommendations in the appendix with the unsupported opinions in Louie's and Jennifer's recommendations.

Effectiveness Tip #4: Put the Recommender in Context
I've seen recommendation letters that state, with obvious pride, "Christina is the most talented undergraduate I've ever taught." That's really impressive if the recommender has been teaching at world-class schools for the past few decades. It's not so impressive if he started teaching last month. Similarly, I often see recommendation letters that don't really explain how the recommender knows the applicant but instead launch right into the writer's opinions. Some recommenders don't have this problem—professors *love* to talk about themselves—but others need to be reminded to introduce themselves in the first paragraph so that we understand why we should take their opinions seriously. Recommenders should also state how long they've known the applicant and how they've gotten to know him or her.

Example:

I am a professor of French Literature at Columbia University. I have been teaching undergraduates and PhD candidates here for eight years. Sarah was a student in my Advanced French class, which we conduct entirely in spoken and written French, as well as my nine-student seminar on Baudelaire, conducted in English. For the latter, Sarah wrote two fifteen-page papers for me, and I also have the privilege of serving as her thesis adviser this year. Over the course of the past year and a half, I have gotten to know her quite well both inside and outside the classroom. She spent at least four hours a week in my classes this year, and she has dropped by my office countless times for discussions about life, literature, and politics. This academic year, we have also been playing squash together at least once a week, and I have been privileged to get to know her on a personal level as well.

Example:

Michelle worked as an intern at the Immigrants Rights Association (IRA) here in San Francisco during the summer of 2003. The IRA is a nonprofit legal clinic that serves low-income immigrants in the greater Bay Area. It is staffed by attorneys on a pro bono basis, as well as by law students, like me, from local law schools including Stanford, Berkeley, Hastings, and Santa Clara. (I am a 2L at Berkeley.) Michelle was one of five interns I supervised that summer, and I was able to review all of her research and written assignments.

Example:

I am a Managing Director at Fancypants Consulting, and I have directly supervised Jeff for the past year, since he was promoted to Associate, a position that usually goes to MBAs from top business schools.

Effectiveness Tip #5: Put the Applicant in Context
The recommender should compare the applicant to his peers and quantify that comparison: "Matthew ranks among the

top 5 percent of undergraduates I've taught in my seventeen years of teaching at Northwestern and Amherst. He is in the same league as one of my students who is currently a Rhodes Scholar, and another who is now doing very well at Stanford Law School."

Many school-specific recommendation forms have grids on them that ask the recommender to compare the applicant to her peers. Here's an example:

	Bottom 50%	Top 50%	Top 25%	Top 10%	Top 1%
Academic performance				X	
Communication skills		X			
Motivation			X		
Maturity				X	
Leadership ability			X		

But the generic LSDAS form doesn't include a grid, so recommenders using that form need to be reminded to put the applicant in context as specifically as possible in their letters.

I've also seen recommendations where the professor praises the applicant's capabilities by saying something like,

"Her research paper on Malory's *Le Morte d'Arthur* was so strong that I gave her an A." So what? For all I know, that recommender gives everyone an A. Why should I assume that earning an A is special, unless the recommender tells me so, and why? Context is crucial. Take a look at the appendix: Madeleine's and Sara's recommendations do a great job of putting them in context.

Effectiveness Tip #6: Weaknesses   Most law school recommendation forms, including the LSDAS form, do not ask recommenders to write about applicants' weaknesses, but it's a subject that can be interesting when recommenders volunteer to discuss it. If your recommenders do discuss a weakness, they should pick one that can be fixed, and explain the steps you are taking to fix it successfully. Examples include budgeting your time better so that you don't wait until the last minute to write your brilliant papers; learning how to deal with project teammates who don't carry their weight; or developing more confidence as a public speaker. Beware phony weaknesses, though. Admissions officers will see right through statements like, "He's too critical of himself," or, "She works too hard," or, "He's too much of a perfectionist."

Effectiveness Tip #7: Stick to What They Know   It really rubbed me the wrong way when someone who had never even gone to law school would write, with utter conviction, that an applicant was "certain to make your law review." (Most schools publish scholarly, student-run legal journals called law reviews, and it can be a prestigious thing to be selected to work on one, depending on the school and the journal.) That's no different than your grandma going up to someone in the supermarket boasting that her little Maggie is certain to be published in the *Journal of Atmospheric and Solar-Terrestrial Physics*. Wouldn't you be hiding behind the produce, cringing in embarrassment? The fact is that even people who have gone to law school and can gauge whether you're suitable for a career in law know that they have no way of predicting whether you'll make law review, not least because different law reviews have dramatically different selection criteria. In my experience, people with law degrees know enough not to venture a guess on law review selection in a recommendation—it's the people who know the least about law school, and law reviews, who do.

A trickier issue is that some recommendation forms express a preference for academic recommendations but then also ask recommenders to discuss the applicant's potential for success in the legal profession. Professors usually haven't attended law school or worked as lawyers, so why they should be expected to have an opinion on that is anyone's guess. Recommenders should feel free to state the limits of their knowledge—if they've spent their entire careers in academia, for example, they shouldn't feel they have to make up some kind of opinion about what it takes to be a good lawyer. On the other hand, if they know something about law school or the legal profession, or can compare the applicant to other students of theirs who have met with success in law school, they should explain how they have that knowledge and offer an opinion about the applicant's prospects.

Effectiveness Tip #8: No (Unintended) Faint Praise "Damning with faint praise"—that's a saying we use to refer to recommendations that on the surface seem to be saying good things but are actually negative because they aren't enthusiastic enough. It's possible that recommenders *intend* to damn with faint praise, but I'm convinced that some don't mean to. If your recommenders show you drafts of their letters, keep an eye out for faint praise like the following:

> Susan is a competent student with substantial potential for law school.
> *Translation: Susan is merely competent, not exceptional, and she's not a sure bet for success in law school.*

> Martin's class work was above average.
> *Translation: Martin was not very far above average.*

> Joseph is very punctual and tries very hard to do his best.
> *Translation: Joseph always shows up on time and works like a dog, but he doesn't have much else going for him.*

> Jessica seems to have an interest in the law.
> *Translation: Jessica only seems to have an interest, but she doesn't really. Or: I don't know her well enough to gauge whether her interest is genuine.*

If your recommenders don't show you their letters, you may never know if they've damned you with faint praise. In the appendix, Louie's recommender from his German II class obviously intended to damn him with faint praise. His translations are "almost always above average in quality," and it was "gratifying to see that he could grasp different parts of speech and understand cases." They met outside the classroom on "at least two occasions," and we learn that he couldn't be bothered to participate in the class field trip "because he had other plans." We also know that "he is looking forward to graduation and the next chapter of his life." The recommender doesn't come right out and say that Louie is lazy and unmotivated and suffering from a bad case of senioritis, but she doesn't have to; that message comes through loud and clear.

How do you avoid that? By asking your recommenders ahead of time whether they feel they can write a superlative recommendation for you, and asking for a candid answer. You're much better off finding out up front than having a tepid recommendation in your file (and never knowing about it).

Effectiveness Tip #9: Length Anything less than five hundred words is too short. If your recommenders really know you well enough to be writing an effective recommendation, and if they are offering anecdotes and not just adjectives, what they have to say should take up more than a page. They shouldn't worry about a letter being too long—if they really know you and are passionate enough about you

to write more than a page, that can only work to your benefit. An admissions officer might not read to the very end—*so
recommenders should put the good stuff first*—but she will
know that your recommender thinks you're someone special based on the time commitment alone. I've rarely seen a
recommendation that was too long—most of them are too
short to be helpful.

Effectiveness Tip #10: Letterhead   Ideally, your recommenders should submit their letters on their letterhead. It
makes clear that they are writing about you in their professional capacities (and not, say, as a friend of the family), and
it makes it easy for admissions officers to track them down
if they have follow-up questions. And that does indeed happen, sometimes because an admissions officer smells something fishy and wants to make sure the letter is legit, but
other times because she just wants to hear more about the
applicant.

CHAPTER 5

Your Life in One Page: The Résumé

Many law schools require or invite people to submit their résumés as part of their applications. I often got the sense that applicants slapped on their résumés as an afterthought. That's a huge mistake. When I settled in to crack open an applicant's file, the résumé was always the first piece of paper I pulled out. What better place to start than a one-page synopsis of a person? Résumés are powerful tools for communicating information about yourself. They don't just communicate bare facts about your accomplishments and experiences; they also reveal a lot about your priorities, what *you* consider important about yourself.

When done right, a résumé also conveys professionalism and polish—that you are presentable and employable, traits that admissions officers have to consider when choosing an incoming class. The applicants they admit are potential ambassadors for their law schools for the rest of their lives, and admissions officers want those people to reflect well on their institutions. For many applicants, this is the first real résumé they've ever put together. For other applicants with more employment experience, the résumé is often a tired piece of paper they've been recycling from one job to the next. Both kinds of applicants need to be mindful of what an admissions officer hopes to glean from their résumés. This chapter offers easy-to-follow rules on how to use your space most effectively, how to give your résumé a professional veneer, and how to make the best impression possible of you as an applicant, future law school student, professional, and alumnus. You'll find models in Appendix D; you can also download them from my website, www.annaivey.com, to use as templates for your own résumé.

THE BIG PICTURE

Here are some big-picture tips before we dive into the nitty-gritty details.

Big-Picture Tip #1: Don't Undersell Yourself People routinely undersell themselves in their résumés. When I interviewed applicants after reviewing their files, I was often surprised to learn about some fascinating interests and experiences that never made it onto their résumés, or anywhere else in their applications for that matter. For example, I once interviewed an applicant who failed to mention anywhere in his application that he was an accomplished cellist. What an important piece of information to leave out! Someone else revealed, after some prodding, that he had written a children's book. "Big deal," you think? Most law school applicants haven't even attempted to write a novel, let alone finished one, let alone found an agent and a publisher. Two other reasons to include something like that: It can play against type if the applicant is, say, an engineer (which one doesn't normally associate with authoring children's books), and it serves as a great icebreaker in interviews.

In this chapter, I'll be discussing different techniques for putting your achievements and experiences in the best light. The chapter is geared toward people who don't necessarily have superstar backgrounds, the folks who haven't been granted multiple patents or won a Rhodes Scholarship. Every top law school receives résumés from people who have done all those things, so you owe it to yourself to make the most of what *you* have done.

Big-Picture Tip #2: Balance With a few exceptions (discussed later), your résumé will have to fit on one page. The way you choose to present yourself on that one page—what you choose to include, and what you decide to leave out—is very revealing. Sure, it's hokey to talk about well-roundedness, and certainly admissions officers care about depth and not just breadth, but nobody likes a one-trick pony, and that's what most résumés suggest about their authors. If a résumé lists mostly academic achievements—Magna Cum

Laude this and Phi Beta Kappa that—I might have great respect for that person as a student and a scholar, but I would also wonder if she has a life outside the classroom, or if she's a grind who never emerges from the library. Ditto for work experience: Is this person all work and no play? Does this person have passions and hobbies? Does he care about other people, whether by way of family commitments or charitable work? Does this person engage with the world when she's not at school or work?

For the purposes of law school applications, your résumé is a snapshot of you as a *complete person*, not just you as a student, or you as an employee or businessperson. Your résumé is a quick way for an admissions officer to see where you went to school, where you grew up, what kinds of jobs you've done, and what you do in your free time. Most applicants think much too narrowly about their résumés. Your résumé should have the following categories, and you should make sure that you give each one its due: Education, Work Experience, Activities, and Personal (I'll go into more detail on each). That doesn't mean those sections all have to take up the same amount of real estate, but you shouldn't forget or neglect any one of them.

These sections might also need to compensate for each other. If, for example, you've been going to school full-time and haven't had a single internship or job, your Activities section had better be brimming over. If you've been working two part-time jobs to put yourself through school, you need to highlight that fact so that admissions officers will understand your lack of extracurricular activities. That also goes for full-time moms: If you've been busy raising a family, say so, and emphasize charitable, community, and other activities in which you've been active.

Big-Picture Tip #3: Play Against Type On a closely related note, playing against type, one of the techniques I recommended for your essay, applies here, too. You want to figure out what kinds of assumptions people will make about you, and play against those stereotypes. Your résumé is the perfect place to do that. So when you're thinking about how to present yourself in a balanced way, try to think of experiences and interests that one doesn't usually expect to find on the same page. Say you come from a notoriously macho environment like stock trading. How interesting it would be, for example, to see a trader who likes to garden, or a librarian who is into Xtreme Sports. Crass stereotypes? Sure. But it's not what most people, rightly or wrongly, would expect from your average trader or librarian, right?

Does that mean you should pad your résumé? I don't mean to get existential, but at the end of the day, nearly every accomplishment that ends up on a good résumé was chosen, among other reasons, *because* it would look good there, and there's no shame in that. You probably decided to go to one school over another because of its prestige, or because you knew you would perform better there. You may have sought a certain job and job title because it would be career (read: résumé) building. There's nothing wrong with approaching activities the same way. It's a fine line, but don't be afraid to use your diverse interests and commitments to your advantage.

This tip does, of course, assume that you *can* play against type. If you've waited until the fall in which you're applying to start thinking about these things, you won't have the time to strategize about ways to make yourself a more interesting applicant and execute that strategy. You can't, from one day to the next, earn a leadership position at a breast cancer foundation. (Of course, you can't become an honors student from one day to the next, either, and this is no different.) It really pays to start strategizing well in advance of your applications so that you have time to find and seize opportunities to make yourself stand out from the pack. It takes a while to build the raw material for an interesting résumé. There's no downside to exploring opportunities that play against your type, whatever that may be. You might hate them, but you might love them, too. Life experience never goes to waste, so if the prospect of your law school applications is what it takes to encourage you to step out of your comfort zone, great! But, no matter what, don't fudge an interest just to seem more well-rounded. If you list sports memorabilia as a hobby, without fail someone will ask you about it. If you list the Red Cross, you should be able to give a credible reason for getting involved. If you're the only guy affiliated with a feminist magazine, expect to encounter—and diffuse—skepticism about your motives.

Take a look at the résumés in Appendix D. Dat Nguyen sure looks like a one-trick pony in the "Before" version of his résumé. It's film, books, some more film, science fiction, and video games. One gets the sense that his entire existence is pretty solitary—there is no evidence that he has any leadership experience, or that he even interacts with other people except on the Internet. In the "After" version of his résumé, we find out that he actually has frontline contact with patients at a medical practice and customers at a bookstore, and that he heads two student organizations.

And look at Shelley Fontenot: She could have presented herself as the typical investment banker/quant jock (as they are affectionately called)—the math background, the CFA certification, and the marathon running are a common profile. But those few lines toward the bottom of the résumé break her out of the mold. Stand-up comedian? Growing up in trailers? Truffaut films? That's good stuff, because it makes her vastly more interesting than your average marathon-running investment banker.

A LITTLE DETOUR

Big-Picture Tip #3 brings me to another important point, one that comes up all the time when I'm counseling applicants and prospective applicants. It's possible that now isn't the best time for you to be applying to law school. Maybe you could make yourself a vastly more interesting applicant if you took a year or two, or even more, to step outside your comfort zone and get that life experience. Applicants are so resistant to the timing issue—they all want to apply RIGHT NOW—but they do

(continued on next page)

themselves a huge disservice if they don't treat the law school application process as a longer-term endeavor. *You have control over how you look on paper.* True, you can't change your résumé overnight. But if you're really serious about wanting to attend the best possible law school, it's worth waiting to apply until you're in top form.

THE EDUCATION SECTION

The Education section should contain, in reverse chronological order:

The Name and Location of Your College or Graduate Program In addition to your college and graduate schools, add any time spent at other schools as a visiting student and any nontraditional programs (post–high school), like culinary institutes or design schools.

University of Virginia	Charlottesville, VA
Clare College, Cambridge University	Cambridge, UK
The Culinary Institute of America	Hyde Park, NY

Your Degree(s) It's customary (and space-saving) to use common abbreviations for degrees, like BA for Bachelor of Arts or PhD for Doctor of Philosophy. If your degree is one that's not so run-of-the-mill, or your school uses less-conventional abbreviations, you can and should use the full name of the degree; otherwise, people might assume that you made a typo or that they're not familiar with your degree. For example, if your school abbreviates Bachelor of Science as ScB rather than the more conventional BS, spell out Bachelor of Science.

The Month and Year You Received, or Expect to Receive, Your Degree   If you haven't earned your degree yet, an appropriate way to designate that is the following:

BA in History expected in May 2006.

Your Major and, If You Have One, Your Minor   If your major isn't well known, you should give a brief explanation in parentheses. For example, some people wouldn't know what to make of majors called Human Factors Engineering or Social Policy, so you need to tell them what that means. Also, make sure that the major you list on your résumé matches what's on your transcript. I've often seen discrepancies. For example, someone might list a major and a minor on his résumé when his transcript lists only a major.

Honors and Awards   Always indicate if you've graduated with honors. If you've been elected to join an honors society, you should use your discretion about which ones, and how many, you list. To an admissions officer, they seem to be a dime a dozen, so if your honors are actually meaningful, you need to educate people about why they're meaningful. Don't assume people know what an Emerging Leadership

Scholar is, what it takes to receive a Dean's Scholarship at your school, how hard it is to be elected to the Phi Alpha Theta History Honor Society, or that graduating "with distinction" at your school means you graduated in the top fifth of your class.

For each honor you list, you should explain how competitive that honor is, or what the criteria were for selection. If membership is purely a matter of a grade cutoff, it doesn't add much information over and above your GPA, and that kind of honor society should be a candidate for cutting if you're looking to make room for other content. You'll have opportunities on the application form to list every single one of these memberships, so you don't need to take up eight lines of precious space on your résumé to indicate in eight different ways that you had a certain GPA. Admissions officers often see many applications from the same schools, or have long experience with those schools, so they'll know if the big honor you're trumpeting is really one that 75 percent of students get, or, as with the John Harvard and the Elizabeth Cary Agassiz Scholarships at Harvard, one that is purely a function of the GPA information that's already on your transcript.

Examples:

Elected to University Honors program, for which about 10% of the student body is eligible; candidates must have a minimum GPA of 3.75 and are nominated by faculty. University Honors students enjoy freedom in constructing their own majors and working closely with faculty on senior projects.

Recipient of the Sonnenschein Award for academic achievement, the highest undergraduate honor awarded at graduation by faculty vote to one out of 2,342 seniors.

Graduated with honors (awarded to top 10% of class and requires an honors thesis).

Your GPA, If It's a 3.5 or Above   If your GPA in your major is substantially better than your overall GPA, or if your GPA improved substantially in the last year or two, you can make that distinction in the following way:

Overall GPA: 3.03 – GPA in major: 3.95

Overall GPA: 3.14 – GPA in last two semesters: 3.80

If you attend a college that does not practice grade inflation (see page 34), you can compare your GPA to the school average. Ditto for majors that are graded more harshly than others at your school.

GPA: 3.45 (schoolwide average is 2.88)

GPA in major: 3.67 (department-wide average in Chemistry is 2.95)

A word of caution: Make sure that the GPA you list on your résumé matches up exactly with the number that appears on your transcript (rather than your LSDAS Report). It looks really bad if you've inflated your GPA or used rounding to your advantage, like writing 3.7 when your transcript says 3.67. People will notice any discrepancy.

Your Class Rank, If Your School Ranks You and You're in the Top 20 Percent or Above   If you're not in the top 20 percent of your class, it doesn't make sense to point out that you're closer to average.

> Class rank: 3/4,075 (top 1%)
>
> Class rank: Top 10%

Do not guess your class rank. List it only if it's official.

Dean's List, If You've Been on It for More Than Just a Semester or Two   Usually, it makes sense to list Dean's List honors only if you've been on it more often than a semester or two. However, if your grades improved over time and you made the Dean's List in the last semester, that's worth highlighting. Otherwise, emphasizing one semester of Dean's List in the past will just make people wonder why you didn't make it more often, or why your grades went down afterward.

The Title of Your Senior Thesis or Honors Thesis   If the title of your thesis or project is too specialized for your average college graduate, or (as has been the trend recently) if the title is humorous or punny rather than descriptive, give a brief description in parentheses:

> Senior Thesis: "Deconstructing Derrida" (an examination of how Derrida's background influenced his philosophy)

Any Substantial Papers You've Written   This can be useful if your major is not in the humanities (say, you're in the sciences, or architecture, or a business program), because admissions officers want to see evidence of good writing skills. A lot of people graduate from college these days without having written a real paper, so it's worth demonstrating your writing experience.

> Substantial papers written: "Giovanni Pico della Mirandola and Italian Renaissance Humanism" (History, 15 pages) and "Mating Rituals in Papua New Guinea" (Anthropology, 20 pages).

Any Graduate-Level Classes You've Taken as an Undergraduate

> Classes included Financial Accounting and Corporate Finance at the Stanford Graduate School of Business.

Classes Outside Your Comfort Zone   If you're an English major, go ahead and mention that you've also taken multivariable calculus—that demonstrates how willing you are to step outside your comfort zone.

> Classes included Multivariable Calculus and Number Theory.

Transfer Information   This is worth adding if you have the room and your transfer was a move up in the world.

> Transferred from San Jose City College after first year.

Information about Junior Year Abroad or Visiting Student Programs   Add your semester or year abroad and tell us what you were studying there.

Clare College, Cambridge University   Cambridge, UK
Spent junior year as a visiting student studying History with an
emphasis on Medieval Britain and Canon Law.

University of Barcelona   Barcelona, Spain
Spent one semester as a visiting student studying Art History.
All classes conducted entirely in Spanish.

Self-Sufficiency If you supported yourself during school
or financed your education, it's appropriate to say so in your
résumé.

Worked 25 hours per week during the academic year.

Financed 75% of my education through part-time work and
loans.

Graduate Programs Applicants who have completed or
expect to complete graduate programs should also list the
titles of their theses or dissertations, along with a description if the title isn't self-explanatory.

THE EXPERIENCE SECTION

This section of your résumé will look a bit different depending on whether you're still in school. If you've already graduated from college and are out in the working world, your
current job should take up the most real estate on your résumé. If you're still in school, you should include informa-

tion on any jobs or internships you've had, whether or not they were paid. Each entry should include the following information:

- The name of your employer, whether a person or an organization

- Your job title

- The months and years of your start and end dates (if you're still working at the job, the end date should say "Present")

- Location: the city and state where you worked

- A sentence or two describing your employer (if not as obvious as, say, Starbucks or the ACLU) and your role there

- Bullet points listing special accomplishments or milestones

This last bullet point, highlighting your special accomplishments, is the most important feature of the Experience section, and people often undersell themselves here. Below are some tips to help you do yourself justice.

Experience Tip #1: Internships—What You Learned Versus What You Did If you've raised $80 million in venture funding for your start-up and grown a company from zero to two hundred people as chief operating officer, good for you! What you did is impressive enough, and you won't have any trouble showing yourself off here. But many law school applicants haven't had spectacular jobs. Most law school applicants haven't risen beyond internships or entry-level professional jobs, and they don't know how to convey what they *learned* (which can be fascinating) as opposed to merely what they *did* (which almost never is). Internships, in particular, are tricky, because you're not there for the purpose of mastering your envelope-licking skills. Rather, you're there to observe and learn something about a particular profession or industry.

I remember one applicant who described in stupefying detail the envelope licking and telephone answering she had done during her internship with a senator in the German Bundestag, the German national parliament, but failed to mention that she had worked exclusively in German or that she had observed interesting differences between deadlocks in the Bundestag and those in the U.S. Congress. (I learned these things only later, during an interview.) That should have gone into a bullet point:

* Worked exclusively in German and observed interesting differences between deadlocks in the Bundestag and those in the U.S. Congress.

That will also give an interviewer—whether in the context of law school admissions or a future job search—a springboard to ask interesting follow-up questions, something that's much harder to do if you've focused on answering phones and filing correspondence.

You can also explain why you sought out the internship:

Sought position to gain experience working for a legislator with a strong record on labor issues.

Sought position to gain finance experience and learn about the investment banking industry.

(Note that to be grammatically correct, this should really say "Sought position to gain experience in finance," but in a résumé, it's appropriate to make small concessions like this to space limitations. See Length Tip #13.)

The same goes for other typical young adult and student jobs, whether it's waitressing at the Cheesecake Factory, whipping up lattes at Starbucks, or babysitting. If you really think about it, you've learned some meaningful skills that every working person needs at any stage in her career. For a waitressing job at the Cheesecake Factory, for example, you really don't need to explain to people what you did. Your broader skills are more important:

Honed multitasking and customer service skills in fast-paced environment.

Guess what? Those are skills that lawyers need, too, and they're worth showing off on your résumé. (Personally, I think a lot of lawyers could use a stint working as food servers—they'd learn a thing or two.) For another example, take a look at the Borders job in Dat's "After" résumé, in Appendix D.

Caveat: If you have a mix of low-level and more meaningful jobs, focus your word count on the more meaningful ones. For the lower-level ones, you can say that you were a barista at Starbucks or a cashier at Phil's Deli and leave it at that. Beef up the lower-level ones as described above if those are the only kinds of jobs you've had or if you have space to fill, and not at the expense of your more meaningful jobs.

Experience Tip #2: What Was Your Impact?   Lots of résumés read like an HR administrator's dream. "Assessed and selected appropriate internal and external resources to conduct ongoing needs assessment." Huh? People write the driest of job descriptions on their résumés without giving us any sense of what they accomplished, what their *impact* was, or how they showed initiative. Quantify wherever possible, and list your most important achievements first. If you picked up or developed good skills along the way, share those as well. In the appendix, Jake's, Dat's, and Shelley's résumés all quantify their achievements, whether in terms of patients served, case documents reviewed, film festival attendance, percentage increase in productivity, or dollar amount of investment banking deals.

Experience Tip #3: Management   If you have any experience managing people, projects, or budgets, say so. And quantify: Tell us how many people and the size of the projects or budgets. If you haven't had management experience, emphasize teamwork experiences, and tell us if you've ever mentored anyone on the job. We learn, for example, that Jake managed paralegals and case assistants, and that Dat managed returns and special orders for a bookstore.

EXAMPLES OF TIPS 2 & 3

Paralegal:
> Oversaw document production and paralegal assignments for one of the firm's largest cases, involving more than half a million pages of discovery material and coordination with 6 opposing attorneys. Honed people and project management skills.

Counseling:
> Oversaw staff of 6 and annual budget of $500,000 to provide clinical treatment to an average of 60 abused children a year. Refined art and music therapy techniques.

Legal Nonprofit:
> Conducted investigations to uncover mitigating evidence in habeas corpus appeals of death-row inmates. My research has been incorporated into appellate briefs in 3 pending cases.

Product Manager for Website:
> Increased monthly site traffic from 150,000 to 250,000 visitors.

Sales:
> Generated $400,000 in new business in my first 6 months.

Consulting:
> Led team of 3 developers to design and implement new accounting software to save client $250,000 in annual costs.

Experience Tip #4: Promotions If you were promoted from one position to a higher one, tell us. And if you know that you were promoted more quickly than others in your position, say so.

> Promoted to Associate after 6 months (compared to company average of 2 years)

> 09/99–05/01   Office of U.S Senator Molly Brown
>   Washington, D.C.
> * Full-time Intern (09/99–06/00). Researched and answered constituent responses involving health care.
> * Promoted to Legislative Correspondent (07/00–05/01). Oversaw all responses to constituent correspondence. Managed 3 interns.

Experience Tip #5: Budding Entrepreneurs If you've been working for yourself, show that off. Running your own T-shirt business or research service is just as impressive (if not more so) than, say, an office internship. List your own business like any other job, like Jake does in the appendix (eBay Star Seller).

> Self-employed T-shirt vendor. Market and sell customized T-shirts and other clothing items to student organizations. Generate net income of $2,000 a month.

> Self-employed private chef. Shop for and cook meals for 2 families 4 times a week. Cook and cater dinner parties twice a month.

Experience Tip #6: Exposure to Legal Issues If your job touches on legal issues in any way, make sure to highlight those. That experience will give credibility to your desire to pursue a law degree.

> Worked with in-house and outside attorneys to oversee and implement changes to company-wide 401(k) plan in compliance with ERISA.

> Consulted with attorneys to ensure compliance with antitrust consent decree in developing newest release of our software.

EXAMPLES OF LEGAL ISSUES

Export controls
Patent applications and infringement
Contracts
Litigation and lawsuits
ERISA and employee-benefit plans
Environmental regulations
Antitrust
OSHA
Taxes
Securities law

Experience Tip #7: Family Businesses Applicants who have worked in family businesses, often since they were kids, tend to understate the skills and experience set they have acquired over the years. Say your family owns and runs a restaurant, and you've been helping out in every part of the business. You could write:

* Waited tables, opened and closed the restaurant.

Or you could think more broadly about your contributions and experiences over the years and write something like the following:

* Learned all aspects of restaurant operations, including hiring and training, inventory management, accounting, equipment leases and purchases, and real estate/lease negotiations.
* Trained and managed waitstaff of between 4 and 8 at any given time.
* Assisted with bookkeeping, payroll, and accounting.
* Helped scout locations for potential expansion.

Dat's experience as an office manager at a medical practice? He was probably working for his dad, but he doesn't have to say that in his résumé. If it's obvious from the business name that you're related, don't worry—it's still real work and you're still learning real skills.

Experience Tip #8: Plain English for Scientists and Consultants Law school applicants with science backgrounds often have trouble succinctly and clearly explaining what they do in terms laymen can understand. It can be hard to switch off all the technical language and detail that becomes so ingrained. Make sure to enlist a humanities friend while you draft your résumé to help you gauge how clearly you are making yourself understood. Most admissions officers' eyes will cross if you talk about nonparametric statistics or confocal microscopy or quantum well states. Consultants face similar challenges: Regular people aren't really sure what you mean when you say you consult on website internationalization and entitlement of content.

Experience Tip #9: Unemployment Unemployment happens to the best of us, and it's nothing to be embarrassed about. You are expected to account for any gaps in your employment after you've graduated from college, so you may as well preempt any questions. You'll need to explain why you were unemployed and what you were up to during that time. The impression you *don't* want to give is that you were hogging the sofa every day with a big bag of Doritos and your Xbox.

> Actively seeking work since being laid off as a result of budget cuts. Using time to improve my Spanish and networking skills.

UNEMPLOYMENT: GOOD AND BAD REASONS

Some examples of acceptable reasons for being unemployed:
- Being laid off
- Caring for a critically ill family member
- Seizing a (meaningful) opportunity to travel

(continued on next page)

And examples of reasons you shouldn't give:

* Personality clash with supervisor
* Hated job
* Caught embezzling, harassing, etc.
* Fired for insubordination

Experience Tip #10: What the Heck? Ours is a wonderfully diversified economy, with all kinds of little nooks and crannies. That's what makes reading thousands of résumés fun...sometimes. You and six other people (including your mom) might know what your employer, Mojo Mercury, does, but the rest of the world won't. Unless you're working for an employer or an organization whose purpose and function is reasonably self-explanatory just from the name, provide a sentence educating us about what the company does—What does it make? What does it sell? Whom does it serve?—before you write your sentence or two describing your job.

9/98–7/00   The Social Venture Group   Boston, MA
Associate Consultant at a consulting firm that serves nonprofits.

Experience Tip #11: Trajectory If the jobs on your résumé seem to jump around without rhyme or reason, you need to inject some. Say you were a VP of Engineering at a dot-com, and the next job you took was as a paralegal at a boutique law firm. That trajectory is not at all self-explanatory, so you should add an explanation like this:

Decided to experience law firm environment before applying to law school.

You might have to find a polite way to explain what really happened. Maybe what really happened was that you were a victim of the dot-com crash, and you're all of twenty-two years old, and there's no chance in hell you'll get a VP-level job at a real company, and so you're getting in line with all the other twenty-two-year-old college graduates for entry-level jobs. You can keep that to yourself and find a diplomatic explanation, like the one above.

Experience Tip #12: Don't Mislead I've seen people write things like, "Chair, Buckwheat College Admissions Office." Really? As a college student? I made an educated guess that that person had chaired some kind of student admissions committee that gave input to the admissions office, answered applicant questions, sat on Q&A panels, and conducted applicant tours and so on. It was probably an oversight, but it sounded pompous and misleading for him to hold himself out as the chair of the admissions committee.

On a more general note, keep in mind that law schools require you to sign a certification attesting to the truth of everything in your applications, and that certification will cover any résumé you submit. There's a line between acceptable fluffing in a résumé and lying—don't cross it. (And, by the way, admissions officers will laugh at obvious fluffing.) Contrast these descriptions for a law firm case assistant, an entry-level job reporting to paralegals and attorneys:

Disingenuous fluffing:

Drafted pleadings and motions and conducted research for attorneys.

Reasonable description:

Monitored court docket for 3 paralegals and 6 attorneys. Organized exhibits for depositions and hearings. Distributed case law updates. Proofread pleadings and motions.

Experience Tip #13: Be Clear Lots of people write things like, "Created analyses in response to research requests." What kinds of analyses? What kind of research? You'll show yourself off to better effect if you use clear language. Use active, take-charge kinds of verbs. Every sentence in your résumé should start with an active verb. Compare:

Provided research assistance

versus

Conducted research

ACTION VERBS

Managed	Oversaw	Researched	Analyzed
Conducted	Advised	Assessed	Developed
Initiated	Spearheaded	Founded	Performed
Coordinated	Trained	Handled	Established
Designed	Investigated	Interviewed	Led

THE ACTIVITIES SECTION

The Activities section is the place for your community and extracurricular activities, as well as any hobbies you pursue through an organization. (Hobbies you pursue on your own, like squash or quilting, will find a home in the Personal section.) Your activities don't have to have their own section—if, for example, all your activities are campus activities, you can create a subordinated entry called Activities under the listing for your school in the Education section. But for off-campus activities, and for activities you've pursued after graduation, it makes more sense to list them in their own section.

Applicants who have already graduated from college and are out in the working world should take care to highlight not just current activities, but also activities they pursued while they were still in school. Admissions officers are trying to put together a class of people who will engage with each other both inside and outside the classroom, and they will look to your activities while in college to try to gauge how involved you'll be with your school and neighborhood communities as a law student. That's why Shelley and Jake both list college activities in the sample résumés.

Many of the same tips that I recommended for the Experience section apply here, too. If you have the room—and you should certainly try to make the room—you should go into the same level of detail for your activities that you do for your jobs. Don't just create a laundry list of your activities, like Dat does in his "Before" résumé. You want to demonstrate your impact. If your role was one of learning and observing rather than doing, focus on what you learned. If you committed a meaningful amount of time to your activities, add the number of hours per week or per month in parentheses (some applications require this for all your jobs and activities). Emphasize those activities where you took a leadership role, had real responsibility, or made an impact. If you have the room, your activities should have start and end dates and locations, just like your jobs (see Dat's and Jake's résumés). And don't assume that other people will know what a particular organization does. If you were involved with Global Campus Initiatives while in school, you'll need to explain what that organization was.

The biggest problem I often see in the Activities section is that applicants just list the bare bones without giving any detail.

Cofounder of Students For Environmentalism
What are the organization's goals? How many members do you have? What kinds of things have you accomplished?

Winner of the 2000 Undergraduate Business Plan Competition
How many people competed? What was your business plan? What are the next steps for your business plan?

Fraternity Fund-Raiser
How much money did you raise? What did your fraternity do with it?

Client Intake Coordinator for Nonprofit Legal Clinic
What kinds of clients did you work with? What kinds of legal problems?

Senior Class Treasurer
Elected or appointed by whom? Do you manage a budget? What size?

Chair, Student Judicial Board
What kinds of cases did you hear? Was the board the final decision maker? Did you also hand down penalties? How did you win this position?

Teaching Assistant, Introductory Calculus
Did you teach? Conduct review sessions? How many students? Did you grade papers? Did you develop your public-speaking skills?

Captain and President of Varsity Tennis Team
How did the team rank? What were your nonplaying responsibilities as captain (team budget, fund-raising, etc.)? How did you become captain (elected by team, appointed by coach, etc.)?

Tutor, Harmony House
What is Harmony House? How many students did you tutor? What ages were they? In what subjects? Were there any particular challenges? Did you achieve any particular success, like helping a failing student raise her grades to a B average? Were there particular challenges, like working with mostly non-English-speaking children?

Take a look at Dat's and Jake's activities—they do a great job communicating their impact. Shelley devotes less space to her activities—she's been working for a while and has to devote a lot of space to that—but she still manages to convey quite a bit.

What if you have so many activities that you can't possibly fit them on a one-page résumé? The best way to decide which ones to cut is to rank them in order of your leadership roles or impact, and then in order of your time commitment—then you can cut starting from the bottom of your list. Admissions officers are very hip to the fact that people sign up for every conceivable activity so that they can fill out this section on their résumés and application forms. Merely *joining* an activity won't get you any credit. Admissions officers want to see that you've made a contribution, that you've taken a leadership role and deepened your involvement in the activity—and that takes time. Listing ten activities with the title "Member" will not reflect well on you (nor will joining a bunch of activities at the end of your junior year, which is very transparent to admissions officers). It will make you look superficial and uncommitted. You're much better off listing three or four really meaningful ones.

Are there activities you shouldn't list? It really depends on the specifics. I remember reading a résumé from an applicant who had listed his participation in a male beauty pageant. I didn't hold it against him, but I thought it was odd, and I was curious to find out what would motivate him to do that. I have also come across activities that really should have been left unsaid. One woman shared, "I have been a faithful reader of *Pen Pal* magazine ever since I began corresponding with inmates." That's too much information.

THE PERSONAL SECTION

The Personal section is really a catchall. It's a place for you to show who you are in your personal life, when you're not at work and you're not at school. Here are the kinds of things to highlight about yourself in the Personal section:

Hobbies and Sports

Make sure you're specific enough. Reading, traveling, cooking, and sports are too general. Being specific allows people to ask interesting follow-up questions. "How did you get into restoring cars?"

Examples:

* Enjoy origami, quilting, Creole cooking, and restoring cars.
* Classically trained pianist since age four; winner of the 1995 Piano Competition for Young People sponsored by the Brooklyn Arts Council.
* Enjoy day hiking, rock climbing, and kayaking.
* Enjoy pickup basketball, flag football, and tennis.
* Three photographs and two poems published in *Organon*, a twice-yearly student-run creative journal with a print run of 1,500.

By the way, don't bother listing "law" as a hobby or interest. I knew people were interested enough in law to be applying to law school, but it always sounded disingenuous to list it as a hobby or interest. If you have a genuine interest in law because of a particular job you had, say, at a legal clinic, or a class you took, then your interest in law will come across loud and clear in the Experience section of your résumé or on your transcript. If the rest of your application doesn't even touch upon the law or things legal, it sounds even phonier to list law as a hobby. Plus, in their heart of hearts, most people would feel sorry for college students who sit around and read law review journals for fun (if one is to believe them in the first place). There's plenty of time for that in law school.

Languages

List every language you've studied or picked up, even if just a little, but be brutally honest about your proficiency. You might end up being interviewed by someone who decides to switch into that language.

* Fluent Mandarin, proficient German, beginner's Portuguese
* Reading knowledge of Hebrew and Aramaic
* Conversational Spanish

Travel

Travel is just as tricky here as it is in the personal statement, just because it tends not to distinguish applicants from one another. Include travel if it was extensive, exotic, or unusual.

* Spent the last two summers trekking through Nepal.
* Spent the summer retracing the route of the *Odyssey* by boat.
* Spent the summer visiting ballparks across the country.

Miscellaneous

You want your résumé to represent you faithfully, and there may be aspects to your life that are important to you and help define who you are but that don't fit neatly into the Experience, Education, or Activities section. These kinds of details are especially important if you want to communicate that you had other demands on your time or special circumstances that make your accomplishments more significant. Examples include:

Growing up in interesting places or with unusual responsibilities
* Born and raised in Guatemala; emigrated to the United States while in high school.
* Attended elementary and high school in Lyons, France.
* Raised on a family farm in South Dakota.
* Have raised two siblings since junior year in high school.

First in your family to...
* First-generation American
* First in my family to attend college
* First in my family to apply to graduate school

Family (this is especially important to add if your family activities take up most of your free time)
* Enjoy coaching my son's peewee football league.
* Go swimming regularly with my two daughters.

OTHER SECTIONS

Other sections can be added as appropriate.

Certifications

This would be the appropriate place for certifications like:

* CFA (Chartered Financial Analyst)—passed all three levels on first attempt
* Series 66 NYSE/NASD Registered Investment Adviser
* American Translator Association: French–English certification
* Licensed insurance agent (Massachusetts and Connecticut)
* Certified teacher, Maine

Anything more obscure than the examples above won't add much value to your résumé. "Cisco Certified Internetwork Expert (CCIE)—Routing and Switching" won't mean anything to this crowd and takes up precious space.

Computer Programming Languages

Most admissions officers will have no idea what PHP is. You can list all your languages, but if some other part of your résumé makes clear that you have programming experience or come from a computer science background, you don't need to list every language you're familiar with the way you would if you were applying for a programming job.

If you do list all your languages, don't pad your list by treating every variation of C++ and every XML language as a different language. If you do, you might get called on it in an interview (not likely, but if an interviewer is familiar with those languages, you'll be exposed as a résumé padder). This should be the first stuff to be cut if you're running out of room—admissions officers just won't be able to evaluate your language set.

Publications and Presentations

If you've been published or have given presentations at conferences, you can list those on a second page under the relevant heading. There is no one particular format you have to use, but your citations should be easy to read and provide enough context if the titles aren't self-explanatory. See Dat's résumé in Appendix D for examples.

The Performing Arts

If you've been a professional performing artist, say, a working actor, you can also use a second page to list your various plays, movies, commercials, and roles. On the first page of your résumé, you can summarize your work experience as an actor and refer readers to the second page.

7/00–5/03   Actor   Los Angeles, CA & New York, NY
Appeared in numerous plays, commercials, and movies. Member of the Actors' Equity Association and the Screen Actors Guild. Please see attached sheet for more detail.

PRESENTATION

The length and format of your résumé are very important.
Very few people spend more than thirty seconds or a minute
scanning a résumé, *so your résumé has to be easy to read or
it won't be read at all.* Here are some tips to help you craft a
reader-friendly résumé.

Unless you have been out in the workforce for fifteen
years, your résumé should not exceed one page. (There are
two exceptions, discussed earlier: publications and public-
speaking engagements can be listed on a second page, as can
performing arts experience.) This is a tough rule to follow,
because if you've been busy and accomplished a lot by the
time you apply, you'll want to show everything off. But you
can't, and you have to prioritize. If you submit a résumé
longer than one page, you will appear incapable of distinguishing between the necessary and the extraneous, a very
important skill for lawyers to have. Also, if you are undis-
criminating about what you include, you dilute the power
and punch of the best material with your weaker accomplishments. No one can admire good muscle tone if it's
buried under fat.

Your résumé will be a lifelong (or at least a career-long)
work in progress. Spending time on your résumé now will
pay dividends for the rest of your working life. You'll need to
revise and reprioritize as you pass through different stages of
your life, but a good foundation will serve you well for years
to come.

Length Tip #1: Contact Information   You don't need to use up five or six lines for your contact information:

Melissa Clark
1659 Branson Street
Bartleby, MI 64502
Tel: (417) 555-4783
E-mail: missyclark@wahoo.com

Instead, you can have your contact information run across the page, and collapse it into two lines:

Melissa Clark   1659 Branson Street, Bartleby, MI 64502

(417) 555-4783   missyclark@wahoo.com

Please, please, please do not use cutesy e-mail addresses. Your contact information is the first thing people see when they look at your résumé, and you don't want admissions officers thinking of you as AbercrombieBabe or Surf-Dude127. The same goes for voice-mail greetings: Make sure that your message is appropriate for professional calls, including ones from admissions officers. A lot of applicants seem to think that "Hey, I'm not in right now, leave me a message" is a professional voice-mail greeting, and I'm telling you that it's not. In fact, no greeting that starts with "hey" is professional. Here's an example of a professional greeting:

> Hello, you've reached Kumar. I'm sorry I missed your call, but if you leave me a message, I'll get back to you as soon as possible. Thank you.

And when the phone rings, make sure to turn down 50 Cent or whatever you happen to have on your iTunes before you answer.

Length Tip #2: References   You do not need to add "References Upon Request" to the bottom of your résumé for application purposes. In fact, you don't need to refer to references at all on your résumé.

Length Tip #3: Objective   Many people use an Objective section at the top of their résumés with a one-line explanation of what they're hoping to accomplish. In the working world, it isn't uncommon to see something like:

Objective: An advertising internship

Objective: A K–12 teaching position

Some law students follow that model and write:

Objective: To gain admission to a nationally recognized law school

Objective: To support my application to law school

As an applicant, you can just skip the Objective section. Admissions officers know why you're submitting your résumé to them.

Length Tip #4: Highlights   In the working world, many people add a Highlights section to the top of their résumés to offer a succinct list of what they have to offer. It's a mini-résumé within the résumé. Here's what it typically looks like:

* Conscientious, detail-oriented, goal-oriented individual
* Excellent interpersonal and teamwork skills
* Exceptional communication skills (writing and speaking)
* Work well under pressure

Since I'm recommending that you flesh out much more of your nonprofessional life for application purposes than you probably would for employment purposes, you will probably find yourself having to cut the Highlights section. Plus, admissions officers don't really pay attention to them. (Most employers don't, either.)

Length Tip #5: LSAT Scores You do not need to list your LSAT scores on your résumé. The admissions officers reading your file will have that information readily available, and you don't need to use up valuable real estate on your résumé to duplicate that information. And don't try to fudge by listing only your highest LSAT score if you took it more than once.

Length Tip #6: High School As a general matter, you don't need to list your high school information in the Education section. Admissions officers aren't usually interested in going back that far, and those who are ask where you went to high school on their application forms. You're much better off using that space to elaborate on your post–high school life. There are some times when it does make sense to list your high school:

■ If you attended a nontraditional high school, like a performing arts high school

■ If the law school you are applying to is located in the place where you grew up but haven't lived in for a while, and listing your high school in your hometown will emphasize your connection to the community and give you credibility for wanting to go to law school there

■ If you went to high school outside the United States

Also, while listing these kinds of high schools is fine, do not take up space with high school activities—you'll look like one of those people who peaked in high school. If your participation in an activity started in high school and continued beyond it, you can list that in the Activities section with start and end dates.

Length Tip #7: SAT Scores   Whether or not you list your high school on your résumé, it is not appropriate to list your SAT scores. The only time your SAT scores are in any way relevant to your law school applications is if you want to argue that you vastly outperformed your SAT score in college and that you expect to do the same in law school despite your not-so-great LSAT score. That argument belongs in an addendum (see Chapter 6). There's no need to bring up your SATs on your résumé.

Length Tip #8: Salary Information In the Experience section, you do not need to provide the name of your supervisor or give your salary information, unless an application specifically instructs you to add that information. What you can and should do is make reference to promotions and raises, such as:

> * Received 50% raise in my first year.

Length Tip #9: Basic Computer Literacy You don't need to list basic programs like Microsoft Word, Excel, operating systems like Windows, or computer skills like Internet research that every college graduate is expected to have mastered. If you've mastered software that is more obscure, an admissions officer will likely not have heard of it anyway.

Length Tip #10: Professional Associations As I mentioned before, an admissions officer is not going to be impressed with mere membership in an organization. If you have a leadership role at a professional association, you should certainly emphasize that in the Activities section. Also, if membership in a particular organization requires certification or a meaningful time commitment—like membership in the patent bar—those should go into a separate Certification section.

> * Member of the Patent Bar: Licensed to practice before the U.S. Patent and Trademark Office as a patent agent. Admission required an engineering or science degree and passage of an exam with a 37% pass rate.

Length Tip #11: Road Not Taken   Do not include information about opportunities you were offered but that you turned down. Here's an example:

University of Nevada   Las Vegas, NV
BA in History expected in 2005 (admitted to Harvard but declined)

Length Tip #12: Redundancy   Be brutal in cutting redundant information. Compare these alternatives:

Completed the implementation of a new billing system.

versus

Implemented a new billing system.

Have been selected as one of two employees to recruit at colleges around the country.

versus

One of two employees selected to recruit at colleges nationwide.

Since joining the firm, have generated $200K in sales.

versus

Generated $200K in sales.

Length Tip #13: Wraparound Sentences   You can find cutting opportunities by looking for sentences that wrap around to a second line. If there are only a few words on the second line, and you can cut just a word or two from the sentence, you'll keep it on one line and free up the whole second line for another entry.

Formatting Tip #1: White Space Make sure there's enough white space on your résumé. If the page is filled with too much text, readers feel overwhelmed and won't bother reading. Your margins should be at least 0.7" on all four sides.

Formatting Tip #2: Fonts Don't get fancy with fonts— stick to Times New Roman or Palatino. Sans serif fonts like Ariel and Verdana tend to be too hard to read. Your smallest font should be no smaller than eleven-point. Section headings like Education and Experience can be twelve-point, and your name can be fourteen-point. Don't abuse large fonts to fill the page.

Formatting Tip #3: Outlining There should be no big blocks of text on your résumé. (See Dat Nguyen's "Before" résumé for an example.) Your résumé should look more like an outline, with different pieces of information subordinated to each other. Avoid full paragraphs of text, and make bullet points your friends. Don't use full sentences; instead, start each sentence with a verb. And you should use different font sizes, as well as bold and italics. The sample résumés in the appendix incorporate all of these elements.

Formatting Tip #4: Consistency Your formatting needs to be consistent across the whole page, so don't switch midstream. If you use "May–Sep '02" as your date format, don't switch to "September '03" or "09/03" farther down. If you're trying to conserve space, the most compact date format is "01/02–09/02." If you add periods at the end of some sentences, you need to add them to all sentences, or take them all out.

Formatting Tip #5: Naming Conventions   Use the two-letter postal abbreviations for states rather than spelling them out:

Boston, MA

Give official names, not nicknames:

St. Petersburg, FL (not St. Pete, FL)

New York, NY (not NYC, NY)

Give official names for schools:

California Institute of Technology (not Caltech)

Virginia Polytechnic Institute and State University
(not Virginia Tech)

Formatting Tip #6: Order of Information   For your application, the sections of your résumé, as well as the information within them, should follow a particular order:

▪ Your name and contact information

▪ Education/Experience:

  • If you're still in school, Education comes after your name and contact information, followed by Experience.

* If you've already graduated, Experience comes next, followed by Education.

▓ Activities:

  * If you're still in school, you can list all your activities here.
  * If you've already graduated and want to distinguish between your on-campus activities and your postgraduation activities, you can subordinate your on-campus activities in the Education section and list your postgraduation activities in this section.

▓ Certifications, if appropriate and space permits

▓ Personal

All items within these sections must be listed in reverse chronological order: The most recent stuff comes first (whether it's a job or a degree or an activity), and then you work backward in time. There should be no gaps in time. Your chronology should be easy to track, and a good way to accomplish that is to put your start and end dates in a dedicated column on the left-most side of the page. Any attempts to obscure gaps in time will raise a red flag to experienced résumé readers like admissions officers.

Formatting Tip #7: Verb Tenses Use the present tense for any jobs or activities that you are still doing currently. Use the past tense for all others.

And, finally, make sure to have a fresh pair of eyes proofread your résumé. Typos in résumés are big, bad mistakes, as they are if they appear elsewhere in your application. Typos inspire the following reaction: "If you can't pay attention to detail when you're supposed to be at your best, what are you going to be like when you're at my school, or when you're a practicing attorney?" Also, every admissions officer is friends with the Office of Career Services staff at their school, and they worry about admitting people who will make the lives of their career services colleagues difficult. If you can't produce a reasonable résumé when you're putting your best foot forward, admissions officers are going to be worried about you as a placement problem down the road.

CHAPTER 6

"Please Let Me Explain": Addenda and
Other Appeals for Clemency

I would like to explain to the admissions committee that my
LSAT score of 157 is not representative of my potential. I am
not a good standardized test taker, especially on the games section, and the test does not measure my other qualities, like my
emotional intelligence and people skills. I hope you agree that
my LSAT score should not prevent my attendance at a top law
school.

A dmissions officers are awash in addendum essays
like this one, in which applicants try to explain or
mitigate something negative in their applications,
whether it's a lousy LSAT score, subpar undergraduate grades,
criminal convictions, or an infinite variety of other liabilities.

But rather than helping their causes, many applicants come off as whiny excuse makers who feel entitled to a free pass. Unless an application requires an addendum (more on that later), more often than not people would be better off saying nothing at all. This is one of the trickier parts of the application. It requires diplomacy, tact, and maturity, all of which are very important to demonstrate as an applicant.

Addenda, when done right, serve an important function. Many applicants make the mistake of using their essays—the part of the application that is supposed to convey something about their personalities or their career goals—to try to mitigate some negative piece of information that appears elsewhere in the application. In doing so, they forfeit their one chance to rise above their numbers and put a personal stamp on their files. So an addendum frees up your personal statement for its intended purpose. And admissions officers really do want to hear from you if you need to explain extenuating circumstances. How are they supposed to know why you barely scraped by academically your freshman year? Was it because you were working forty hours a week to help support your mom and little brother after your dad skipped town, or was it because you were a lazy slacker who spent more time hitting the bong than the books? Admissions officers aren't mind readers—some things you have to tell them. So this chapter covers the most frequent "negatives" that applicants typically want to explain, and offers advice on how best to handle them.

LSAT SCORES

I know that the LSAT is the bane of every applicant's existence. I hated the games section, too. So you have trouble figuring out that the green bead fits in the second slot behind the orange bead on the eight-beaded necklace in less than twenty seconds. What does that have to do with your ability to parse the Copyright Act or draft a will, you ask? Beats me. I fully appreciate your frustration if you suspect the LSAT is holding you back as an applicant, but there are appropriate ways and inappropriate ways to communicate that frustration to admissions officers. Most I've seen are inappropriate. *If you're in doubt about whether to submit an addendum about your LSAT score, you're probably better off refraining.*

LSAT Tip #1: Don't Tell Them How to Do Their Jobs Admissions officers are professionals who are trained, among other things, to interpret LSAT scores. That's their job. They know what the LSAT measures and what it doesn't. Much as you may disagree with the value of the test, they care about what it *does* measure, or they wouldn't require it. But they also know that it doesn't measure emotional intelligence or people skills; you don't need to point that out to them. If you want to highlight all your wonderful attributes and skills that aren't captured by the LSAT, point those out in your résumé and your essay.

LSAT Tip #2: Why Should They Believe You?   The LSAT score is designed to predict how you'll do academically in your first year of law school. If you want admissions officers to believe that your LSAT score isn't gauging your academic potential accurately, you need to persuade them. You can't just tell them as much, like the applicant at the beginning of this chapter, and expect them to take your word for it. As an aspiring lawyer, you need to marshal the evidence and make your case. I have seen *only two* truly compelling arguments:

▪ That standardized tests consistently underestimate you, and you have the track record to back you up. If you bombed your SATs, for example, but are in the top 10 percent of your class at a highly competitive college, you can argue that the LSAT is similarly flawed in predicting your success in law school. If that describes your situation, you should submit a copy of your SAT or ACT score report along with your addendum.

▪ That English is not your first language. Admissions officers understand that, all else being equal, nonnative speakers have a tougher time getting through the test as quickly as native speakers. If you think your LSAT score does not represent your abilities accurately because English is not your native language, it's appropriate to point that out in an addendum.

On the other hand, there's a rich variety of *lousy* reasons that people routinely offer to admissions officers, and they are the subject of this chapter's remaining LSAT tips. Why are most of them lousy? Because you have the opportunity to cancel your score if you think you bombed it or weren't at peak performance for some reason. If you don't cancel, and leave your score on the record, you can hardly expect admissions officers to discount them. The Bad Addendum in Appendix E makes this common mistake.

As of the time this book goes to press, you have two options for canceling your test score: You can fill out the cancellation section of the LSAT test form before you leave the test, or you can submit a written cancellation request that LSAC must receive within nine calendar days after your test date.

LSAT Tip #3: Illness and Other Catastrophes

I know that my LSAT score is considerably below your median. Unfortunately, I came down with strep throat/my mother was in a life-threatening car accident/I was struck with insomnia the day before the exam, and because December was the latest date I could still take the exam and apply to your law school this year, I was not able to cancel that test and retake it at a later date.

There are plenty of legitimate reasons for botching your LSAT exam. Lord knows most of us wouldn't be able to perform very well on a standardized test under these kinds of circumstances. However, the fact that you waited until the last possible date (December) to take the test—that you basically took the chance that something would happen and you wouldn't be able to retake it—shows a stunning lack of foresight and planning on your part. If you find yourself in this kind of situation, you're better off canceling your score and delaying your applications until the following year rather than applying in the current year with a crummy LSAT score and—to make matters worse—an addendum that highlights your lack of foresight and your bad judgment.

LSAT Tip #4: Acts of God and Human Error

I took the LSAT in Malibu, California, and the proctors did not stop the exam during the 3.7 earthquake on October 5. I was too distracted to perform as well as I otherwise would have.

The proctor called time on one of the sections five minutes too early.

There was a jackhammer right outside the window of the gymnasium throughout the entire exam, and the proctor did nothing about it.

There are so many LSAT tests being administered all around the world, it's no surprise that things sometimes go awry. And proctors, who are given the discretion to handle unusual testing circumstances, are only human. Every test date, I'm chained to my phone, because the calls come pouring in from my admissions counseling clients with complaints (some justified, others not), and the calls pour into LSAC as well.

LSAC has appeal procedures in place to deal with these kinds of situations. You can call them up right after the test to report unusual testing circumstances like the ones above (based on true stories, by the way). If their own investigation persuades them that the testing was indeed compromised, they can do anything from offering people the opportunity to retake the test without penalty on a different day, to including with your LSDAS Report (at your request) a notation that explains the unusual circumstances. If LSAC does not agree with you or anyone else who complains that the testing was compromised, you still have the option of canceling your score and retaking the test. Here's the important part: *If you choose not to pursue either avenue, you don't have any compelling grounds to ask admissions officers to discount the validity of your score.*

If LSAC offers to let you retake the test, I recommend that you do so rather than have your score submitted to law schools with an explanation of the bad testing circumstances. You would effectively be asking admissions officers to guess how you might have done under normal testing conditions, and they're not omniscient. You're better off retaking the test and giving them a score that doesn't require X-Men superpowers to interpret. (Plus, they don't get to put an asterisk next to those scores for the rankings.) And hold off on that addendum until you see what your second score is. You're inviting admissions officers to laugh at you if you do the same or worse when you retake the test.

LSAT Tip #5: Ignorance

I know your policy is to average multiple LSAT scores, but I request that you disregard my first LSAT score because I had the flu and left halfway through. I didn't know at the time that it was possible to cancel the score, and by the time I found out, the cancellation deadline had passed. If I had known, I would have canceled, and you would have only the more recent score.

This excuse just makes you look bad. It's your responsibility to understand what the test-taking rules are, and the test form itself gives you the option to cancel. Lawyers can get disbarred for missing deadlines and failing to understand procedural rules, so an addendum of this nature does not inspire confidence in your future as a practicing attorney. It also demonstrates that you didn't care very much about the test taking or the application process if you couldn't bother to read the instructions.

LSAT Tip #6: Learning Disabilities

I have a learning disability and can't perform on the LSAT as well as other people.

My psychologist recommended to LSAC that I be granted 5 times the regular time limit for each section of the test, but LSAC turned down my request. After I sued them under the Americans with Disabilities Act, we settled out of court on a compromise of 2.5 times the regular time limit for each section. Because I was granted only half the extra time I had asked for, my score is not an accurate one.

I have trouble processing words quickly, and I have been diagnosed with a learning disability, but I did not apply for accommodation on the LSAT test. I ask that you take my learning disability into account when you review my test scores.

If you have a learning disability, you should have it documented by professionals and seek testing accommodation from LSAC. If LSAC doesn't agree that you need accommodation, you won't persuade a law school that you really deserved special treatment. A law school is not going to conduct its own investigation into the nature of your disability—schools don't have the expertise or the budgets or the time—and it is not going to second-guess the professionals at LSAC who specialize in that assessment. And if LSAC did accommodate you, you have even less credibility in arguing that your score doesn't measure you accurately enough.

GRADES

Explaining an aberration in grades lends itself much better to addenda than LSAT scores. Very few people make it through college without going splat once in a while, and one often suspects that people who don't go splat didn't push themselves beyond their comfort zones. We all know people who take the path of least resistance—the ones who take the easiest classes and sign up for meaningless, undemanding activities. Top law schools aren't interested in those applicants, and they want to see some academic risk taking. (Of course, admissions officers still want their GPA medians to be as high as possible, but all else being equal, they want the person who chose the harder curriculum.)

Grades Tip #1: Grading Curve   Grades don't mean anything outside of context, so if your school doesn't offer a lot of context on its transcripts, you should provide it yourself, assuming it works in your favor. If your school's average GPA is a 2.9, your 3.3 looks much more impressive than it would, all else being equal, at a school with an average GPA of 3.7. Or maybe you're taking a particularly tough major with a draconian grading curve. That is valuable information that you should point out to admissions officers. Some colleges are more accommodating than others about providing this kind of information to their students. It's worth a dedicated attempt. Also note that *LSAC photocopies only the front of the transcript for your LSDAS Report.* If there's an important explanation on the back of your transcript, such as why there's an asterisk next to one of your grades, or what the grading system means (if it's not A-B-C-D-F or 0–4) then send an explanation or send a copy of the explanatory notes on the back of your transcript. And if your registrar or your academic dean has a system for converting your grading system into the typical four-point scale, that conversion would be useful to include. Admissions officers will appreciate it.

I receive plaintive e-mails all day long from anxious engineering and science majors who worry that their grades are being stacked up against the poli-sci kids. Admissions officers understand that engineering and the hard sciences typically apply much tougher grading policies than majors in the humanities. But they won't necessarily know, for example, if your school's philosophy department is famous on campus for its harsh grading. And they also won't know if your 2.9 average in your physics major is above the department average. If you have access to that information for comparison purposes, you should share it, or have your recommender address it.

Grades Tip #2: Wrong Major Some people have trouble in the first few years of college because they picked majors that turn out not to be a good fit for them. Typically, the people who write these kinds of addenda were pre-med majors who hit a brick wall in Organic Chemistry, realized that they didn't want to be doctors after all, and had knock-down, drag-out fights with their parents before switching to liberal arts majors. That story is so common that admissions officers can recognize it at a glance just by looking at your transcript. If you're nodding your head at this story, you don't need to write an addendum.

One trap that a lot of people fall into here is to suggest that the reason they didn't do so well is because they weren't passionate about the subject matter. Passion, shmassion. Law school, indeed, life itself, is full of tasks and assignments and responsibilities that are hard to get passionate about, but that doesn't give you an excuse to blow them off or put forth less than your best effort. If your grades weren't so hot because you couldn't get excited about your major, make sure to emphasize that, in hindsight, you understand that that's not a legitimate approach to your academics and your work going forward.

Grades Tip #3: Wrong School   Other people flounder the first couple of years because they picked the wrong college, or their parents forced them into the wrong college. Matching high school students to the right colleges—colleges where they'll be happy and thrive academically and socially—is very hard, and students are pressured to attend particular schools for all sorts of bad reasons that end up condemning them to four years of misery and malaise. Perhaps they decide to transfer to another school, where they end up thriving, or they decide to stick it out and make the most out of the situation. If you fall in the former camp, you don't need to write an addendum, because admissions officers will spot your improvement once you switched environments. If you fall into the latter camp, though, it would help admissions officers to understand the source of your difficulty. You need to give some thought to your stated reasons, because you don't want to tell one of the smallest law schools in the country, for example, that you felt suffocated in your intimate college setting.

Grades Tip #4: Age   Just about every college admits people who are a bit younger than typical applicants. Some of those prodigies adapt and prosper in college right away, but others really suffer from the age and maturity gap. They may have the smarts to hack it academically (otherwise, they wouldn't have been admitted at their age), but their social lives can be very difficult. And as college students of all ages know, when your private life suffers in college, your academics are usually not far behind. If you took a little time to land on your feet in college because of your unusually young age, don't be afraid to speak up and be candid about your difficulties adapting to college life, and be specific about how you succeeded in turning things around.

Grades Tip #5: Course Overload   There are college students who, for one reason or another (usually financial), load up on as many courses as possible every semester so that they can graduate quickly. Some people pull off this strategy with aplomb, while others end up spreading themselves too thin and compromise all the courses they're taking and activities they're participating in.

Grades Tip #6: Course Underload   Some college students can't take a full course load every semester and need more than four years to complete their degrees. Unless told otherwise, an admissions officer will just assume that you decided to go easy on yourself. So, if it took you longer to graduate for a good reason—family illness, Division I sports commitments, financial difficulties, or health problems, for example—make sure to explain why.

Grades Tip #7: Goofing Up and Goofing Off   Maybe you don't have a good excuse for those lousy grades in your earlier college years. Maybe you were really bright but went hog wild, goofing off with your newfound freedom. If you got your act together and turned your academic life around, some self-awareness mixed with contrition can work in an addendum, but don't pretend you have an excuse.

Grades Tip #8: Language Difficulties   Many law school applicants learned English as a second language, and for some people that transition is easier than for others. This addendum makes the most sense if you are explaining difficulties in your past. If your language difficulties are more recent, this is a trickier proposition, because you don't want to create doubts about your ability to keep up in law school. If you are still facing language challenges, your best bet is to demonstrate that you're executing an aggressive strategy to get your English up to speed by taking relevant classes.

Grades Tip #9: Entrepreneurship   It's not uncommon to see people blowing off their academics to pursue entrepreneurial ventures. While it would be better for those folks to have taken some time off from school to give the entrepreneurial life a whirl, or waited until they graduated, for some people that advice comes too late, and they're stuck with bottom-of-the-barrel grades and (more often than not) an equity stake in a business that never got off the ground.

Entrepreneurship is a beautiful thing, and it's one of the things that makes this country great. But law schools aren't looking for entrepreneurs. They like entrepreneurs, and they're happy to have entrepreneurs in the student body, but first and foremost they're looking for people who can handle the rigors of the law school curriculum. As with any addendum explaining lousy grades, your task is to persuade admissions officers that your lousy transcript is not an accurate reflection of your capabilities. This kind of addendum should emphasize all the terrific skills and life lessons you learned in your entrepreneurial quests, and how they are going to make you a better law student and lawyer. Admissions officers want to know that if you decide to take a job during law school, or if you're going to be working all day and going to school at night, you'll be able to keep your grades up while you juggle your different commitments.

Grades Tip #10: Family Responsibilities The stereotypical college student is still a kid, blissfully unburdened by family responsibilities, indeed, the beneficiary of their parents' family responsibilities. But life doesn't always work that way, and even applicants who are the typical college age (late teens, early twenties) sometimes have families or other people to support for one reason or another. Some are already married and have spouses and children to support. Others help support and raise siblings or take care of ailing parents or grandparents. These kinds of family responsibilities often make it difficult for people to devote as much time to their studies and extracurricular activities as they would like. For some, these responsibilities are temporary and affect only a semester or two, but other people find that their family responsibilities affect their entire college experience.

In either event, you should educate admissions officers about those responsibilities so that they can put your grades and extracurricular activities into context.

Grades Tip #11: Financial Responsibilities   There are those lucky folk who don't have to worry about the cost of their college educations. Good for them! Many other applicants have to assume all or part of their expenses, however. I've seen applications from people who worked full-time jobs while attempting a full-time course load in college. More often than not, the college side of that equation suffered. It is very important for applicants in this situation to explain what kind of work schedule they were bearing in college and why. And if you're in that situation now and still have time to do something about it, consider taking time off from school so you can save up some money. No admissions officer will fault you for that.

Grades Tip #12: Difficult Transition   Maybe you're not a child prodigy or supporting a family or languishing at the wrong school. Perhaps you've found the right major, and the right school, and you're taking the right number of courses, but you had a really tough time making the transition from high school to college. That's not unusual, and it's an explanation that admissions officers understand. Not everyone lands on her feet freshman year, and some people just take longer than others to hit their stride while they're adjusting to a very different life. As long as you've turned your performance around, it's worth telling this story.

Grades Tip #13: Health Problems Grades can take a nosedive when people confront long-term health difficulties. A whole semester, if not more, can be swallowed up by a case of mono, not to mention more serious ailments like cancer. These kinds of health problems are appropriate to point out in an addendum, but be careful about raising red flags about problems that may be recurring, like depression, chronic fatigue, and the like—problems that could make it hard for you to get through law school and find and sustain a job afterward. Under the law, admissions officers are not allowed to take this into account when deciding on your application, but why plant the idea in their heads in the first place?

Grades Tip #14: Death and Illness in the Family As if college and that time in one's life weren't difficult enough, some college students have to deal with the illness and death of close family members. Aside from the fear and grief and emotional toll that those situations take, many students also have to travel great distances, sometimes commuting across the country on a regular basis, to help family members deal with doctors' visits, painful treatments, financial strain, as well as home care and funeral arrangements. Sudden but temporary dips in their transcripts are easily understood when those circumstances come to light. Take a look at the Good Addendum in Appendix E for an example.

Grades Tip #15: Learning Disabilities It is not uncommon for applicants to point out that they have learning disabilities, usually ADHD or dyslexia. Federal legislation bars schools from discriminating against people because of their disabilities, and all schools that I know of have university-wide policies to the same effect. If your college accommodated you, it's probably not a good idea to write an addendum, because your school already did everything it could to level the playing field for you. It makes sense to discuss learning disabilities in an addendum only if you weren't diagnosed (this is more common with older applicants, before disabilities testing became ubiquitous) and therefore weren't accommodated.

Make sure to emphasize the techniques you've mastered to compensate for your learning disability. Admissions officers read many addenda from people who explain that the reason they did poorly in college was because they have trouble reading quickly or processing the written word. Law school, of course, requires hours and hours of speed-reading every day, and the practice of law involves reading and writing under crushing deadlines. Law students without learning disabilities have trouble keeping up with the reading load in law school, so you have to forgive admissions officers if they wonder to themselves how these applicants will manage in law school and in legal practice. They can't deny you because of your disability, but you should anticipate those concerns and address them head-on.

Grades Tip #16: Incompletes, Withdrawals, Etc. Don't write an addendum to complain about how LSAC calculates your grades—especially if your complaint centers on the fact that your college let you retake a class you flunked and expunged the old grade but LSAC won't. That kind of addendum just draws attention to the bad grade on your transcript, and makes admissions officers think that you can't take responsibility for having screwed up the first time.

Grades Tip #17: Divorce   Addenda about divorce are also very common. Many applicants have suffered emotionally, academically, socially, and financially—their parents were so busy fighting the War of the Roses that they didn't notice how their kids were coming unglued. You should certainly tell your story if your grades suffered, but understand that you're a member of a very large club.

Grades Tip #18: Abusive Relationships   Sadly, there are applicants whose grades suffered in college because they were abused, either physically or emotionally. I've read addenda, for example, from women who stopped going to classes altogether because their abusive boyfriends wouldn't let them out of their sight for even an hour, and they were too embarrassed to be escorted to class by these stalkers.

The law school application process requires people to turn around and look at their past, a hard thing to do for people who have left behind painful episodes, moved on with their lives, and want to stay focused on the future. As much as you may dread revisiting those experiences, you should explain what happened so that admissions officers understand why you weren't able to do your best in college.

Grades Tip #19: Substance Abuse Problems The transcripts of people with substance abuse problems in college never emerge unscathed. There are people whose problems went way beyond partying too hard—students who had to be hospitalized for liver diseases, who dropped out for semesters at a time to feed their addictions or to attend rehab, who can't remember huge chunks of their college years. It is difficult and painful to write this kind of addendum, but you really have to if an admissions officer is to have any hope of understanding what you were going through. Society has come a long way in de-stigmatizing addiction. That won't lessen the pain or the embarrassment you may feel in writing your story, but know that most admissions officers will try to understand what you went through, and in most cases they'll admire you for confronting your problems and getting clean.

Again, as a matter of federal law, schools aren't allowed to discriminate based on addiction (which is considered a disability), but you should still allay realistic concerns that people will have about your ability to handle the pressures of law school and legal practice. Make sure to demonstrate how you've conquered your demons, even if that means (as it does for all addicts, I'm told) that your battle with those demons will be a lifelong proposition.

REQUIRED ADDENDA

Most application forms will ask you point-blank whether you were charged with or convicted of criminal misdemeanors or felonies, and if you had any disciplinary problems (academic or otherwise) in college or graduate school. You must disclose these, and you must be honest. And if you're not sure whether you need to disclose something, err on the side of disclosure. Here's why: Application forms all make you attest that you're telling the truth, the whole truth, and nothing but the truth. If you are later found to have been dishonest in your applications, you can be kicked out of law school and prevented from practicing law. So tell the truth, even if only out of self-interest. The best way to handle the criminal and disciplinary addenda is to disclose, show remorse, and prove that you've changed.

STYLE

Your tone and word choice are very important in addenda. Because you're asking admissions officers to discount or overlook very important parts of the application, you run the risk of sounding as if you are

- Groveling

- Whiny

- Arrogant

- Irresponsible

- Immature

- Lacking in good judgment

- Lacking in self-awareness

Here are some tips on ways to couch your plea in the most effective, least off-putting way.

Style Tip #1: Length   Most addenda can say what they need to say in two pages, double-spaced. In fact, most can be quite a bit shorter. If you had mono the second semester of your freshman year, you don't need more than a paragraph or two to convey what happened. The only addenda that should exceed a couple of paragraphs are the ones that are very personal, like ones involving abuse or addiction or grave family difficulties. Remember that these kinds of addenda are unsolicited—you are basically foisting something on an admissions officer that he didn't ask for and requesting that he spend more time reviewing your application than he does other people's. Make every word count, or you'll really test his patience.

Style Tip #2: Show Deference to Their Expertise   Make sure you don't use language suggesting that you're telling them how to do their jobs. Rather, make clear that you're just supplementing the information in the rest of your file.

> I know that you have a lot of experience evaluating transcripts, but I would like to share some context in case you are not familiar with the particular grading policies and class requirements of my major.

Style Tip #3: Clarification Requests   Invite them to contact you if they have any questions or need clarification.

Please don't hesitate to contact me if you need more information about this matter.

If you would like to see copies of my medical records from that time period, I would be happy to forward them to you.

Style Tip #4: Don't Oversell Your Case Stating your case too forcefully also signals that you're telling them how to do their jobs—the language suggests that there is no room for disagreement.

I think it is obvious that my LSAT bears no relationship to my true ability to succeed in school.

Clearly, I am a much better student than my transcript suggests.

Style Tip #5: Don't Overstate Your Flaws Overstating your flaws suggests that you won't be able to handle the pace and pressure of law school. You won't get to keep canceling and retaking that six-hour take-home Property exam, for example.

I became so flustered during the reading comprehension part of the test that I lost my concentration for the remaining two hours.

Style Tip #6: Don't Pat Yourself on the Back Too Much Don't go overboard praising yourself.

Although tempted to take the easy way out and buy the cheap ticket to success, I always took the harder courses, always challenged myself in a way my peers did not, even if that meant lower grades.

Style Tip #7: Avoid Melodrama   Even people who are suitably restrained and professional in the rest of their applications can take things a little far with the rhetorical flourishes when they're writing addenda. There is much beating of the breast, donning of the hair shirt, and wailing and gnashing of teeth. People love to talk about the "sweet success of that hard-earned B–," "the bitter pill of failure," or their "unforgivable, abject failure to study." Take a look at the Bad Addendum in Appendix E for more examples. You're better off sticking with simple, straightforward language.

Style Tip #8: Don't Make Demands   You are not in a position to demand things of admissions officers, especially where their staffs and budgets are concerned.

> Because I was diagnosed with dyslexia after I finished my college education and took the LSAT, I believe that a trained expert should be consulted by the admissions office on the subject of whether my college grades and LSAT score are fair reflections of my abilities.

Style Tip #9: Too Much Information   Unnecessary detail detracts from the important part of your message. Contrast the following examples:

> Because I had terrible asthma and bronchitis as a child—I was hospitalized in the winter of 1978, the summer of 1982, and

again in the winter of 1983—I missed a lot of basic math training that I needed in my freshman calculus class in college.

versus

I have always had difficulty with math, but I didn't realize how much I needed to brush up on the fundamentals until I received a very disappointing grade on my calculus midterm.

During the final, I felt a sharp ache in my back, which slowly started radiating into my chest and legs. Then the stomach cramps kicked in like exploding fireworks and I had to leave five times during the test to run to the bathroom with diarrhea.

versus

I experienced acute muscle pains and stomach upsets during the final as a result of what turned out to be the onset of the flu.

Style Tip #10: Remorse and Lessons Learned   Be direct, and don't suck up. Start your addendum with something straightforward, like, "I would like to share with you some information to help you evaluate my transcript." And make clear that you learned something from whatever unflattering or difficult events you're writing about.

In hindsight, I should have taken a leave of absence from school while I was tending to my mother in her last few months.

If I could do my freshman year over again, I would do quite a few things differently. That experience taught me not to become complacent just because I had performed so well—and so effortlessly—at my previous school. I will guard against that temptation in law school.

I have no excuse for my slide into alcoholism, and I will be spending the rest of my life ever vigilant against the temptation. I would give anything to go back in time, and I have many amends to make with the people I hurt along the way.

Style Tip #11: Stop While You're Ahead If you have multiple reasons for your less-than-stellar performance, stick to the most important one. Throwing in everything but the kitchen sink makes you sound like you blame everyone and everything but yourself for your performance. For example, it may very well be the case that you picked the wrong school and you were getting your first taste of independence from your parents and you were diagnosed with ADHD, but it wouldn't be a good idea to belabor all those problems in your addendum.

And don't make excuses for multiple parts of your application. If your grades, LSAT, and résumé are all poor indicators of how you'd do in law school, how are admissions officers supposed to decide on your application? If everything about your application needs an excuse, how often are you going to be in the dean of students' office when you're in law school?

OTHER UNSOLICITED MATERIALS

I've seen it all. And heard it all. And smelled it all. I've listened to applicants' karaoke tapes on my commute home. Examined still-life photographs. Thumbed through dissertations. Are most admissions officers this curious? No, not even close. Most unsolicited materials like this don't even make it into admissions officers' hands—they're just not interested. The administrative staff might have a good laugh, though.

Will these kinds of materials hurt you? Not if your submission is in good taste. A professional quality audition tape showing off your classically trained voice or acting monologue won't hurt you. Your grainy, black-and-white studies of high-rise buildings using solarizing darkroom techniques won't hurt you. But anything even mildly outré or un-PC probably will. So, no satirical newspaper columns referring to cripples, and no audition tapes for *The Vagina Monologues*. There's just no way to know whether your file is going to be read by someone who shares your cutting-edge sense of humor or your comfort with body parts and words the FCC bans from the airwaves. Also, if a law school instructs you not to submit unsolicited materials, don't.

The corollary: Always assume that admissions officers might read, listen to, or watch anything that shows up in your application. If you list your web page or blog, assume that they might go check it out. If you list a URL, be prepared for admissions officers to see what's there.

As for dissertations, senior theses, science fiction novels, and other tomes, remember this saying: *Admissions officers dread the files that land with a thud.* It is entirely sufficient to list the title and subject matter of your work on your résumé. If an admissions officer really wants to read your oeuvre on representations of women in the salons of revolutionary France or your experimental vowel-free novel set in the year 3064, she'll ask for a copy.

CHAPTER 7

The Thirty-Minute Audition:
The Interview

I once interviewed a woman with an LSAT score in one of the lowest percentiles possible—ordinarily a rejection for a school like Chicago. On a hunch, I brought her in for an interview, and ended up admitting the person with the lowest score in the law school's history. Her presentation skills were impeccable, she spoke articulately, and her recommendations were flawless. More important, though, were her persuasive skills. Like a seasoned litigator, she gathered her evidence and persuaded me that her LSAT score was simply wrong as a predictor of her law school performance. Talk about wow factor! I would not have taken that kind of risk, however, without interviewing her first.

On the flip side, I've also endured the nervous allergy sufferer who shredded so many tissues during her interview that flakes ended up in her hair, the guy who kept scratching himself where he shouldn't have, the gal who droned on for twenty minutes about the minutiae of her senior thesis on irrigation systems, and the guy who announced, "You're late!" when I walked into the room. One guy kept showing up in my office for weeks after our interview until I finally had to call security on him. And another looked deep into my eyes and recited his favorite love poem.

Applicants clamor for interviewing opportunities, because they want that extra chance to impress admissions officers. They all assume that they would do themselves a favor interviewing, because, you know, *everyone's* a great interviewer, just as everyone's a great poker player and a great driver. How wrong they are. Most people aren't born on this earth with great interviewing skills. It's a learned skill, and it takes time and practice. That's *good* news, because that means that you, too, can become an ace interviewee.

Chicago is one of a minority of law schools that offer admissions interviews, so I was one of a few admissions officers who had the pleasure of conducting them. Of the top fifteen or so schools, for example, only Chicago and Northwestern invite people in for interviews. If admissions officers lived in a perfect world with unlimited time and unlimited budgets and unlimited staff, they would interview every applicant before making a decision. Sadly, we don't live in a perfect world, so most schools will get to know you only on paper. Don't despair, though, because you can take advantage of important opportunities for "stealth interviews" with schools that don't offer formal admissions interviews. We'll cover both types, in turn.

OFFICIAL ADMISSIONS INTERVIEWS

There are four primary reasons why some law schools spend their time, effort, and budget on admissions interviews.

Reason #1: Self-Selection You know, and I know, and law schools know that most people pick a range of law schools based on rankings and location, and then they send off a bunch of applications. I've worked with clients who, against my strenuous advice, applied to thirty or even forty schools. And since applications have moved online, it has become that much easier to shoot off those extra two—or twenty—applications (and somehow they manage to cough up an extra $800 in application fees, no small thing).

The rising number of applications per applicant puts law schools in a tight spot. Because of the way the rankings work, and because they have to predict how many people will accept their offers, schools don't want to waste offers on people who won't accept, so they try to find ways to determine who really, really, really wants to attend their school. Bottom line: If you receive an interview offer and don't go, you can expect the thin envelope.

And don't assume that this rule doesn't apply to you just because your numbers might be very desirable for a particular school. In that case, they might very well assume they're just a safety school for you and that you're likely to get in somewhere higher up the food chain. They won't want to extend you an offer unless you demonstrate your sincere interest and show them some lovin' by coming in for an interview.

And what if you don't have the kind of cash it takes to fly out for an interview? If you want to stay in the running, charge it and get a job over winter break. You can use the opportunity to check out the school, something that applicants should do anyway before deciding which offer to accept.

Reason #2: More Information   If the law school extends interview offers by invitation only (as opposed to schools like Northwestern that extend interview opportunities to all), it might do so because they're not sure yet which pile you belong in. Maybe you're what's called a "mixed predictor" (see page 17): You have a great LSAT score but a lousy GPA (or vice versa), and they want to hear you address that weakness to their satisfaction. Or your numbers are okay but not great, and they don't want to extend an offer unless they're convinced you'd sell your firstborn to attend. Or you're a legacy applicant, and they're extending you an interview opportunity as a courtesy because it would be too awkward to reject you right off the bat.

Reason #3: Recruiting   Admissions officers want an opportunity to market their schools to you. They are gatekeepers, but they're also in sales and marketing. If they do end up making you an offer, they want to have had a jump-start on recruiting you. Some law schools that offer interviews are absurdly bad at the marketing aspect, but the smart ones seize the opportunity to sell themselves.

Reason #4: Weeding Out the Duds   If a school selects you for an interview (as opposed to schools that have open-door interviews), they ultimately want to find out if you're a likable, interesting person. It's really that simple. They called you in because they didn't want to reject you outright, because there was something about you on paper that they really liked. Calling you in for an interview is basically a way for them to confirm whether their gut instinct about you was right. Keep in mind, though, that even schools with open-door interview policies will be turned off by duds in the interview—they do plenty of weeding out at this stage, too.

The people who fare poorly in this scenario are the people whose numbers were good enough to be spared rejection, but who weren't interesting enough, on paper at least, to merit an offer. If those people aren't dazzling and interesting and bright in their interviews, either...Ding! On the other hand, for people who are called in because their numbers are only so-so but their essays and recommendations and life experiences made the admissions officer sit up and take notice, it would be hard for them to blow their interviews unless they turn out to be total duds in person—not very likely.

What kinds of things do admissions officers like to see? There's no hard-and-fast rule, or a secret list—most of it is gut instinct—but here are some qualities that interviewers care about:

■ Maturity

■ Self-awareness

■ Honesty

■ Energy

■ Speaking skills

■ Personality

■ Appearance

■ Attitude

■ Professionalism

■ Creativity

■ Sense of humor

Of course, most people are a mixed bag, and the person who is eminently professional and mature might not be the wittiest, and the creative person might not be the most polished. That being said, there's one quality that every interviewer wants to see: Energy. You want to sparkle with energy and good attitude when you walk into that room. I remember an applicant who spoke about a mile a minute about some bug he had been researching. He spoke way too fast, and he kept abandoning his sentences in midstream.

Above all else, he sounded *young*. But his enthusiasm was palpable, and I couldn't help but think how much I would love to see him getting this excited about the law.

Interview Tips

So, what does the typical interview look like, and what's the best way to prepare?

Interview Tip #1: The Interviewer Lottery You may not get to interview with an admissions officer at all but rather with an alumnus, a staff member from another department like career services or alumni relations, a current student, or someone who was hired just to conduct interviews. Increasingly, schools that still offer interviews are outsourcing them to people outside the admissions office so that admissions officers can read files. Alumni interviews are the trickiest to predict—there is much less quality control, because alumni don't conduct admissions interviews on a full-time basis, and they're basically volunteering.

Unless a school is going to pair you up with an alum, in which case you'll probably find that out ahead of time, you won't know until you show up for your appointment whether you'll be meeting with the dean of admissions, someone lower down the admissions food chain like an admissions director, or someone entirely outside of admissions, like a staffer from career services or a current student. If you had a say (which you don't), you would prefer to go as high up the food chain as possible, because the dean of admissions doesn't have to lobby other people in admissions to admit you if she decides you're the bee's knees.

As much as you may be tempted to grovel or cajole or pull strings to land an interview with the dean of admissions, don't. Groveling and cajoling won't get you anywhere, and you will annoy the admissions staff to no end. As for having strings pulled on your behalf by some muckety-muck who knows a professor or went to kindergarten with the provost, believe me when I tell you that there are few things more irritating for the dean of admissions than feeling bullied into interviewing some snot-nosed, spoiled brat who gets special privileges because of his connections. And you really don't want to alienate the dean of admissions.

Interview Tip #2: Depth of Knowledge The nature of the interview—the kinds of questions asked, the knowledge that the interviewer will have about your file, the interviewer's knowledge about the school—can vary dramatically depending on the kind of interviewer. Some interviews are conducted "blind," meaning the interviewer won't have seen your file at all before you show up with your résumé in hand. She won't know that you scored a 176, or that your economics professor worships the ground you walk on. Other schools have their interviewers read the files beforehand so that they can drill down into more nuanced detail in their conversations with applicants.

Some interviewers will have worked at that law school for decades (maybe even went there as law students) and can answer all your questions about the school and then some, but others will have been hired the day before and won't be able to tell you squat. (Unfortunately, those interviewers also won't be able to recognize that you're the perfect match for that school even when the perfect match is sitting under their noses.)

Schools who invite anyone and everyone to come in for an interview usually offer the least substantive interviews. Because of their open-door interviewing policy, their interview volume is very high, and they just can't offer the same depth in interviewing as the schools that select only a fraction of applicants for interviews. The open-door interviews can be very frustrating. Worst-case scenario, it goes something like this: You show up and fill out a form on a clipboard with your basic stats, after which an admissions counselor looks at your form and your résumé, asks a few questions about your background, tells you that your LSAT is on the low side, and thanks you for coming in. *And you flew all the way across the country for that?* I can't tell you how many calls I receive from frustrated applicants venting about how much money they spent for an assembly-line interview. I tell them all the same thing: These interviews are tests to see who really wants to attend, and if you don't care enough about the school to go in for an interview, the school won't "waste" an offer on you. That's life.

Interview Tip #3: Length Most law school interviews last somewhere between twenty and forty minutes. Alumni interviews tend to run longer than interviews with admissions officers, because alums aren't interviewing applicants all day long.

Interview Tip #4: Softball Interviews Most interviews are of the softball variety. The interview will feel chatty and friendly and pleasant. The softball interviewer will ask some icebreaker questions to put you at ease and get the ball rolling, like, "Where did you fly in from?" and will try to find something interesting in your file or on your résumé to bond over. If you discover that you're both huge fans of the Pittsburgh Steelers or *The Pirates of Penzance*, run with it.

Interview Tip #5: Hardball Interviews Hardball (or stress) interviews are a dying breed, but you'll encounter them in different stages of your career, so you may as well learn how to handle them with panache.

Hardball interviewers won't ask you friendly icebreakers or help you get comfortable. Instead, hardball interviewers want to see you squirm. They'll ask you inflammatory and aggressive questions designed to undermine your confidence, and they want to see whether you dissolve into a puddle or fight back. You *should* fight back. Don't get emotional. Don't get huffy. Don't act offended. Instead, fling your own zingers right back at them, with a smile. You have to act as if you're enjoying this little game. It's a macho interviewing style, and it rewards macho responses. It's designed to see how you handle yourself under pressure.

Remind yourself that this is a test, and that the answer you give is not half as important as the way in which you deliver it. And by all means, don't take anything personally, even if you think the aggressive interview goes too far, that it steps over a line.

Women and men tend to fall into different traps here. Men risk sounding blustery and defensive, or they come off as arrogant and disdainful rather than effortlessly confident. Men are also far more likely to employ a certain brand of sarcasm and belittling response tactics, which won't serve them well. Women, on the other hand, are more likely to have their passion misinterpreted as emotional and shrill.

Here are some examples of hardball questions so that you know them when you see them.

"So, I see on your résumé that you have dual citizenship. That's illegal."

"It's obvious that you signed up for all these extracurriculars because you thought they would look good on your résumé."

"Your essay argues against limitations on greenhouse gases. You don't really believe that, do you?"

If you encounter a hardball interviewer, keep your cool, and don't cede your ground.

Interview Tip #6: Froot-Loop Interviews While most admissions officers stick to straightforward softball interviews, every once in a while you'll get an interviewer (usually an alumni interviewer) who spent a little too much time getting baked back in college. Or at least it will sound that way. They'll want to know what kind of tree you would be if you could be any kind of tree, or what kind of animal you want to come back as. Or they'll ask you weird dichotomies, like, "Triangle or square?" Or your name is O'Malley and they'll ask you if that's a Swahili name. And before you can say "New Age hocus-pocus" three times, *the interview is over.* It's the famous Proust Questionnaire gone horribly, horribly wrong. Honestly, I wish I could tell you how to handle these kinds of questions, but there's really no way to prepare for them. Just keep certain thoughts (like, "Are you on crack?") to yourself, and go with the flow.

Interview Tip #7: Practice   Here are some typical questions you're likely to encounter:

- Welcome! Have a seat. Where did you travel in from?

- How did you like your college?

- How did you pick your college?

- Did you enjoy your major?

- So, tell me about your current job/internship.

- Tell me about that master's degree/senior thesis/research project.

- Tell me about your volunteer work.

▪ So, you figure skate/bowl/grow bonsai trees!

▪ What else do you do in your free time?

▪ What good books have you read recently?

▪ So, why law school?

▪ Why do you think you want to study law here?

▪ What questions can I answer for you?

Know your résumé cold—it will likely be the source of many questions. All that hard work you put into molding your résumé into a promotional piece will pay off here. Your statement of purpose will come in handy, too.

Painful as it may be, go to your career services office, or borrow your buddy's camcorder, and tape yourself doing a mock interview. Notice your facial ticks, your verbal ticks, when you're speaking too quickly, when you're speaking too slowly, when you're looking up too much, when you're looking down too much, when your eyes are shifting nervously, when you're slumping in your chair, when you're saying "like" six times in every sentence, when you're mumbling, when you're shouting, when you're rubbing your palms on your pants, and when you're twirling your hair. If you need to, lock yourself in a room with a consolation bowl of popcorn to review your mock interview on tape. You can always burn it afterward without anyone having to know (just don't inhale the fumes, because you'll need those brain cells for Contracts).

Interview Tip #8: Important Points In your mock interview, practice answering the questions by making your most important point first. You never know when an interviewer is going to cut in, and you never know if you'll have a chance to go back to the point you were trying to make.

Interview Tip #9: Stay on Message Go in with an agenda. What are the two or three core messages you want to communicate about yourself? What is your marketing strategy? Maybe you want to communicate that you've risen above your ten-year-old college transcript, and that your leadership skills and real-world experience set you apart. Or that a law degree, combined with your science background, will allow you to make a great contribution to health-care policy. Ask yourself: What do I want this interviewer to take away from this meeting? What are the two or three most compelling reasons to accept me? When this interviewer sits down with the rest of the admissions committee to make her case for admitting me, what are the most compelling arguments I want her to make?

Especially in softball interviews, you'll have plenty of opportunities to steer the conversation in the directions of your choice. For example, you'll be asked plenty of open-ended questions ("I see you have a background in medical research—tell me a little about that."), and those are invitations for you to get your core messages across.

And never, ever answer a question with one word or one sentence. If someone says, "Where did you fly in from?"

don't just answer, "Oakland." Instead, work in important information that communicates your excitement about that school, like, "I flew in from Oakland—I'm a senior at Berkeley. I'm so excited to be back in New England, though, because I have family in western Massachusetts, and I'll get to see them on this trip." If you answer with a single word or a nod, you will have lost (in this example) a chance to convey that you have important family ties to the area and that you'll therefore be more likely to accept an offer.

Similarly, if someone asks, "Did you enjoy your time at FSU?" don't say, "Yeah, it was okay." Instead, you can demonstrate that you've reflected on your education and this formative period in your life, that you're capable of mature self-analysis, and that you can convey your opinions diplomatically:

> I'm so glad I went to FSU. I know the size of the school is not for everyone, and it can be easy for some people to get lost in the shuffle, but from the get-go I made it my goal to form relationships with professors, and I feel very privileged to count some of them among my friends and mentors.

Or:

> You know, at first I had to find my bearings, because I felt pulled in so many different directions. Did I want to pursue chemistry or philosophy? Did I want to continue throwing myself into theater, or did I want to try something completely new? I decided I wanted to try new things, and, of course, I re-

alized that I liked some disciplines and activities far more than others. In hindsight, I'm glad that's the approach I took. I never would have discovered a love for the Classics if I hadn't decided to experiment.

Interview Tip #10: Take Control   Just as learning how to give knockout interviews takes time and experience, so, too, does the art of interviewing people. The odds are good that you'll run into someone who hasn't mastered it yet. A common rookie mistake for interviewers is to hog your airtime. A good interviewer will do about 25 percent of the talking, but there are people out there who will spend the entire interview yakking about themselves or their lousy commute or your suit or their golden days in law school. If you feel your interview time slipping away, take back control of your airtime. Don't interrupt him in midsentence, but look for a natural break in the conversation to jump in.

Interview Tip #11: Questions   There's a 99 percent likelihood that the interviewer will conclude by asking if you have any questions for him. Always have at least two questions prepared. If you don't ask your own questions, you'll be sending a very strong signal that you're not very interested in that school. When you're preparing your own questions, don't ask anything obvious, or anything that's answered on the website or in the viewbook ("What is your student-faculty ratio?" or, "What's your placement like on the West Coast?"). Also, try to ask open-ended questions—they are wonderful opportunities to learn something about the school. Here are some examples:

▪ How do you see the school changing in the next five years?

▪ What do you think are the law school's greatest strengths? And its greatest weaknesses?

▪ What do you think are the greatest misconceptions about the law school? What surprises students the most when they show up as 1Ls?

▪ I see you have a great placement rate for federal clerkships. Are there particular judges or circuits that this school is known for?

▪ How would you characterize your students? Is there a particular personality type that fits in well here? What kind of person is happiest here?

Now, don't expect the interviewer to have answers to all these questions. Sadly (for both you *and* the law school), many of them won't know the school well enough. But even if you don't get answers to these questions, you will have served an important purpose, because your intelligent questions will demonstrate your thoughtfulness about your decision to apply to law school in general and to that school in particular.

On another note, don't feel as if you have to save all your questions for the end of the interview. A good interview is a dialogue, with a lot of questions flowing back and forth. Feel free to ask questions throughout, but don't be pushy, and stay cognizant of the fact that you still want to be doing 75 percent of the talking.

Interview Tip #12: Weaknesses You may very well have been invited in for an interview because there is something in the liabilities column that gives the file reader pause. In that case, unless it's a blind interview, the interviewer will probably come out and ask you about that GPA or that academic probation, or whatever. *Don't hide your weaknesses if they come up.* Instead, find a way to spin them in your favor. And if your liability was of the nature that can't or shouldn't be spun (say, you have a drunk-driving conviction), address it head-on and show that you've changed. On the other hand, don't dwell on your weaknesses, either. Tackle them and move on to something positive.

And don't do what one of my interviewees did. He had a great LSAT score—considerably above our median—and interesting work experience and extracurricular activities. And I loved his essay, which was just oozing with personality. There was only one problem: his lousy GPA. He hadn't written any kind of addendum addressing that weakness, and I wanted to hear what he had to say about it. In the interview, I asked him point-blank about his GPA, explaining that it was considerably below our standards. Not only did he fail to answer my question, but on top of it, I detected a faint hint of annoyance that I had even asked.

He wouldn't have had to say very much to allay my concern. I suspect his explanation would have taken all of three sentences, something like, "I know my GPA, on its face, looks low, especially for a school like Chicago. But that number by itself doesn't communicate that I was majoring in a very difficult engineering program at a school known for its rigorous engineering programs, and I actually graduated above the median GPA for my major." Boom. That's all it would have taken. Instead, I got nothing but attitude.

There's an even sadder ending to this story. He decided to hop on the Princeton Review discussion board and debrief everyone about how his interview went. He gave the full blow-by-blow, and surmised that I had really liked him. So on top of his less-than-stellar GPA, he also lacked any kind of self-awareness or emotional intelligence. Ding!

Interview Tip #13: First Choice Don't be afraid to communicate to a school that it is your first choice (if indeed it is your first choice). Make reference to conversations with current students or alums—mention them by name—to demonstrate that you've done your homework and haven't applied on a whim. Do not, however, tell a school it is your first choice if you have said the same thing to another school, or if you still have a binding early decision application pending at another school.

Interview Tip #14: No Whining I don't care how bitter you are about your college experience, or how justified you are in hating your job. No bitching and moaning allowed in interviews! Nobody likes a constant complainer, and sounding too negative will make an interviewer worry that you'll end up bitching and moaning to the world about her law school if she lets you in. There are plenty of techniques to signal your feelings diplomatically.

Say someone asks how you enjoyed your college experience. Instead of saying, "It was a total party school, what a bunch of meatheads," say, "In hindsight, I would probably choose a school that focused more on academics and less on Greek life, but I got a great education and made the most of my opportunities." Instead of saying, "That school is just way too large, I feel like I've lived at the DMV for four years," say, "It's a large state university, and in hindsight, I think a smaller school would have been a better fit for my personality, but I got a great education, and I didn't have to go into a lot of debt." And if someone asks you why you left what looks like a very promising job, instead of saying, "My boss couldn't manage his way out of a paper bag and makes PMS jokes to boot," say, "I enjoyed having the opportunity to develop my management skills—I had four people reporting directly to me—but the culture of the firm was not the right one for my personality, and it was the right time to explore other opportunities."

Interview Tip #15: Other Schools   You may be asked what other schools you are applying to. That's a tricky question, because where else you apply can be very revealing.

Personally, I don't think it's a fair question, and it's nobody's business but your own. But if they ask, you can't say, "Mind your own beeswax." I would name those schools that have something in common with the school you're interviewing with. For example, if you're interviewing with a school in the Midwest, name your other schools in the Midwest. If you're interviewing with a top-ten school, name other top-ten schools. What you don't want to do is present them with a list that looks scattered, that doesn't have some kind of readily defensible organizing principle. And you don't want to look unconfident, for example by naming mostly second-tier schools to an interviewer for a top-ten school. Also, don't ever say anything bad about another school. First, it's unprofessional, and your judgment will look bad. And, second, your interviewer may have gone to that school.

PRESENTATION

As with most things in life, whether it's term papers or first dates or interviews, presentation matters just as much as, if not more than, the content of what you say. Social psychology experiments have shown that most people subconsciously make up their minds about you within thirty seconds of meeting you, sometimes just from a handshake!

Presentation Tip #1: Polish   Part of what interviewers are judging is how you'll come across in a law firm interview and to the larger world beyond law school. They don't want to make an offer to someone who's going to have trouble landing a job because of his terrible presentation skills. (Every major law firm has lawyers who are deadly smart but can't be let out of the back office because they look like they sleep on a park bench.) And they don't want to make an offer to someone who will, as a student and alum, scare applicants away at their admitted-students recruiting events. The person who interviews you will be asking herself: What will this person be like as an alum? Will he reflect well on us? Do we want him as an ambassador for our school for the rest of his natural life?

Presentation Tip #2: Confidence   Confidence is key to a good interview, and you have to project it even if it doesn't come naturally to you. And nobody wants to be represented by an unconfident lawyer. So whether you're marching into an interview or a courtroom or a negotiation, you have to go in there expecting to knock 'em dead. You want to walk into your interview projecting that you are serious about your career, that you know exactly where you're coming from and where you're headed, how you're going to get from point A to point B, and how Law School X fits into that plan... *even if* you don't really feel that way. If you can't project that kind of focus and determination, you're not ready for the big leagues yet. Don't go in with the attitude that the interview, let alone your education or career, is something that's happening *to* you. If you doubt whether you can project that kind of confidence because you're just not that optimistic or confident a person, go out and read Martin Seligman's *Learned Optimism*. One of the great insights of cognitive behavioral psychology is that you can "fake it till you make it," and you can learn how.

On the flip side, you don't want to come off as arrogant. Never give the impression that a school is your safety. You have to give the impression that you're thrilled to be there and that you'd be honored to receive an offer. Remember: You aren't entitled to an offer, and you have a lot of competition. Even if, in your heart of hearts, you have already come to regret spending the $70 to apply, once you walk through that door, it would be rude and unprofessional to treat your interviewer with anything less than respect, if for nothing else than spending her time listening to you.

Presentation Tip #3: Sales Skills Closely related to confidence: Be ready to sell yourself. I sometimes asked people point-blank why they thought I should extend them an offer or what they would add to the mix of the entering class, and I can't tell you how often I was met with stunned silence. People would just sit there, looking at me like deer caught in the headlights, wiping their sweaty palms on their laps. And after what felt like an eternity (to them and to me), they would reply, "You know, I didn't really prepare for that question." *What did they think the interview was for?* (I remember one woman I had just interviewed hopping on the Princeton Review site to complain how I had expected her to sell herself. See a pattern here? Watch what you say in online forums. When I was an admissions officer, I used to read them all the time, and I wasn't the only one.)

Bottom line: You have to be your own best advocate, and you have to be willing to toot your own horn. Women, especially, tend to undersell themselves. This is an important life skill, and you'll hold yourself back if you don't develop it.

Presentation Tip #4: Happy, Sunny People In interview situations, there is a strong bias in favor of extroverts. It's unfair, but that's life. So if you're a natural-born introvert, learn how to fake extroversion. Think of a good friend who's an extrovert, and channel that person. You can bear to be chatty and exuberant for half an hour. Speaking of exuberance, keep in mind that sounding professional doesn't mean you have to be boring or humorless, so don't be afraid to laugh. You want to leave your interviewers wanting to spend a lot more time with you, preferably another three years.

Presentation Tip #5: Miscellany

- Don't sit until invited to.

- Refer to the interviewer formally (Dean Johnson, Ms. Taylor). Switch to first names only if asked.

- Make regular eye contact.

- Make sure to answer the questions they're asking. Listen carefully.

▓ Don't finish their sentences or cut them off.

▓ Look for cues that they want to change direction or change
the subject. Come up for air so that you don't ramble.

▓ Don't swear, even mildly.

▓ Don't refer to any women over the age of seventeen as
girls.

▓ Always introduce yourself with a firm handshake, and
ask how the interviewer is doing.

▓ Make sure you know your interviewer's job title and last
name.

▓ At the end of the interview, thank her for her time. Ask
her for her card, and send her a thank-you e-mail the
same day. (A handwritten note would be more proper,
etiquette-wise, but snail mail takes too long.)

▓ Be nice to staff. Chat them up. Learn their names. They
can make your life very pleasant or very difficult.

Presentation Tip #6: Sound Like an Adult   Another reason to tape yourself doing a mock interview is to hear
whether you sound like an adolescent or an adult. Count the
number of times you say "like" and "sort of" and ban them
all. Make sure you speak loudly enough to hear, and (women,
especially) don't make all your sentences sound like questions. ("I want to go to law school? Because I want to be a
prosecutor?") This is not the time to start channeling Drew

Barrymore. Make sure you speak in complete sentences. Use correct grammar, things like "good" versus "well," "I" versus "me." And don't drone on and on and on, as if you have verbal diarrhea.

Presentation Tip #7: Appropriate Attire You don't want people to notice you or remember you for your clothes or your hairstyle. I'm not saying that you can't be your crazy, wacky self in other situations, just that it's not appropriate—or helpful to you—in this one. If you're dressed professionally, your clothes won't stand out.

For men, that means:

▨ A wool suit, preferably 100 percent wool

  ✦ Your jacket should be single-breasted.
  ✦ Worsted wools are best for warm weather, gabardines and flannel wools for colder weather.
  ✦ You should be able to button your jacket without the buttons bulging.

▨ A blue, white, or neutral long-sleeved dress shirt (buy the wrinkle-free kind)

▨ A tie, preferably 100 percent silk

  ✦ No novelty ties, and no bow ties, unless you're George Will.

▨ A leather belt

  ✦ The color should coordinate with the color of your shoes.

■ Polished dress shoes in black or burgundy

■ Dress socks

  * The color should coordinate with the color of your trousers.
  * Socks should be long enough so that we don't see any skin between your shoes and your cuffs when you cross your legs.

■ Facial hair should be very conservative.

 For women, that means:

■ A suit

  * Wool is always appropriate, but there are also a lot of great synthetics out there these days—you can roll them in a ball and throw them in your suitcase, and they still look like a million bucks when you unpack.
  * Pantsuits are fine if you don't want to wear a skirt.
  * Skirts should not be any shorter than two inches above the knee.

■ A blouse or a shell (silk or faux silk) or a knit, fitted turtleneck

■ Polished heels or flats in black, navy, or a neutral (no open toes, and heels shouldn't be higher than two inches)

■ Nylons in a color that matches your skin or that coordinates with your black or navy shoes (always have a spare pair with you)

- Understated (if any) jewelry (pearls, small gold or silver studs or hoops, wedding/engagement rings only)

- Makeup should be understated (no bright red lips, only neutral eye shadows, no glimmer)

- No dagger nails or colored nail polish

For both men and women:

- Black, navy blue, gray, and neutrals are always appropriate suit colors.

- Don't buy something that kinda-sorta fits just because it's on sale.

- Avoid linens (too wrinkly).

- Use a three-way mirror when you're trying on clothes.

- Sleeves and hems are easy and relatively cheap to alter.

- Skip the cologne and perfume—it's too easy to overspray, especially when you're nervous.

- Make sure to wear enough antiperspirant.

- Pop a mint just before your interview, and don't forget to take your allergy medicine if you need it.

- Don't smell like smoke.

If this is all bewildering to you, make your way over to a Macy's, Bloomingdale's, Lord & Taylor, Nordstrom, or Brooks Brothers, ask a salesperson to help you pick out a conservative interview suit, and make sure to have the store alter it for a good fit. Men can also find great interview suits at Men's Wearhouse, despite the cheesy ads. Tell them your budget up front so they can steer you toward the right selection. Men should expect to pay $300 to $500 for a good suit, and women should expect to pay $200 to $400. A good suit is a great investment—you'll get plenty of wear out of it during law school when you're interviewing for summer jobs, competing in moot court, and attending splashy events. If in doubt about what a conservative suit looks like, check out the men's and women's suits at www.brooksbrothers.com.

LOGISTICS

Last but not least, keep these logistical tips in mind when you're scheduling your interviews.

Logistics Tip #1: Time Slot   Ask for the earliest slot in the day, and if that's not available, choose the latest time slot. People are more likely to remember you that way. Also, you don't want to compete with their rumbling tummies or their midafternoon nap-time energy slump.

Logistics Tip #2: Time of Year   Find out when that school's students are taking exams or on break and schedule around those weeks. If you're traveling all that way for an interview, you may as well get a sense of what it's like to be a student there.

Logistics Tip #3: Job Title If you have the choice, interview with someone from the admissions office rather than an alum.

Logistics Tip #4: Order of Schools Schedule your safety schools first—you want practice before you interview at your top choices.

Logistics Tip #5: Open-Door Schools For schools that allow any applicant to request an interview, you're better off scheduling your interview for a time after your essays are at least complete, even if you haven't sent them in yet. Your essays will force you to articulate many of the messages you'll want to communicate in your interview, and you should have a good sense of how you'll be presenting yourself in your application, particularly in your statement of purpose, before you head in for an interview.

Logistics Tip #6: Directions Get very specific directions on how to get there and where to park. If you're flying in, find out what airport is most convenient. (Most school websites provide this information.) Arrive at least fifteen minutes ahead of your interview. If you arrive earlier, use the time to wander around the law school.

Logistics Tip #7: Extra Résumé   Bring a copy of your résumé with you in case your interviewer can't find her copy.

STEALTH INTERVIEWS

So, are you just out of luck if the school of your choice doesn't offer admissions interviews? Not at all. You just need to take advantage of what I call stealth interviews. You actually have plenty of opportunities to meet and chat with law school representatives. Each year, admissions officers travel all over the country to attend law school forums (see www.lsac.org for a complete schedule), where they talk to thousands upon thousands of people to answer their questions. They also visit many colleges around the country to meet with undergraduates interested in law school. Law schools also offer information sessions and open houses for prospective applicants on campus. (You can find their schedules on their websites during the fall.) And if they can't make it to a forum or school, they usually send a current student or an alum.

Stealth interviews can be just as effective as formal interviews for making a good or bad impression. When I was traveling for Chicago, I took all kinds of notes on people I met at colleges and law school forums. I had my own little system of symbols that I put next to people's names on my sign-in sheets. The woman at the Los Angeles forum who impressed me with her presentation skills and career goals? I stayed in touch with her and made her an offer. The guy at the D.C. forum who kept invading my personal space by inching his way back behind my side of the table? Ding! The woman who was rude to our financial aid adviser at an information session? Ding! The guy whose mother did all the talking at my forum table? Not necessarily a ding, but definitely not a good impression, either. Of course, I couldn't remember everyone who crossed paths with me, but I had no trouble remembering the names and faces of people I really liked and the ones I really loathed. If you introduce yourself to an admissions representative, understand that you're making an impression that might last.

And a final tip: If you do talk to an interviewer, alum, or other law school representative who is clueless or arrogant or crazy or loathsome to you in some way, don't hold that one person against the school. I'm sure your college is, as we speak, being represented somewhere by someone who would make your toes curl, too. Every school has some bad apples, and you owe it to yourself not to write off what might be a great match because of one clueless admissions officer or bitter alum.

CHAPTER 8

Prestige and Price Tags:
How to Pick a Law School

People apply to law school with different personal goals and preferences in mind, but there are some things that all applicants should think about as they explore where to apply and which offer to accept.

PRESTIGE

I don't need to tell you that there's a big difference between going to Harvard Law School and going to barely accredited Podunk Law School. But things can get tricky when, for example, you've been offered a full ride from Boston University and zip from Harvard, or you know you want to practice law in Manhattan and you're considering Santa Clara versus Syracuse.

You've already heard my reservations about the *U.S. News & World Report* rankings of law schools (see page 20), but they do offer a useful shorthand for thinking about and referring to certain tiers within the great food chain of law schools in discussions like these, especially when you combine them with other rankings and your own research. Please keep in mind that when I refer to, say, the "top fifteen schools," I don't mean literally spots 1 to 15 in the rankings this year (and the rankings do change pretty frequently— much more frequently than those institutions really improve or decline in real life). All I mean to convey is a certain *ballpark* in the rankings, and I don't mean to exclude whoever happens to be ranked 16, 17, or 18 this year. On top of that, the rankings can be way off base for a particular school that they consign to the wrong ballpark, and there are always exceptions to generalizations like the ones I make below.

There are a couple of good reasons to choose the top fifteen, besides bragging rights. Their degrees are much more portable, because those law schools are truly national, even global. Their student bodies come from all over the country and the world, and their graduates are players on the national and global job markets. You could easily graduate from Penn and work for a top firm in L.A., just as a graduate of NYU has no trouble landing a spot with an international firm in Hong Kong and a Cornell grad can work for a legal clinic in Chicago. On the other hand, a graduate of Brooklyn Law School is really looking at the New York/New Jersey/ Connecticut market, and if, for example, you're certain you want to be working in San Francisco after you graduate, it doesn't make a whole lot of sense to get a degree from Vermont Law School, even if you are a bit of a ski bum. That said, in my experience it's hard for people to be certain where they will want to end up after law school. You might end up meeting a soul mate from Atlanta and want to move there after graduation, in which case you'll have a tough time marketing your Brooklyn Law degree.

In terms of geography, the only time a degree from a regional school might make more sense than a national degree, all else being equal (including finances), is if you know you want to go into politics in your home state and need to be wheeling and dealing and schmoozing the locals from the get-go, and you know that the locals will take offense that you went off to that fancy-pants school across the country when our local schools are just fine, thank you very much. For example, I would counsel someone who wants to run for office in Louisiana to turn down the top fifteen in favor of LSU.

The top fifteen also offer a level of job security that other law schools can't. People at the top schools who find themselves in the middle of the pack or even below still do just fine on the job market, even at the highest levels of the job market. The further down the food chain you go, though, the less of a safety net you have. Once you get to the second tier and below, you need to be at or near the top of your class to end up at a top firm in your region or with a top judge in your region (the national market is a much more difficult proposition), and people in the bottom half of the class often face grim hiring prospects. That's one of the reasons graduates from those schools are more likely to hang out their own shingles for solo practices. There's nothing wrong with solo practices, but it's not the same as working for Cravath or the DoJ (U.S. Department of Justice, pronounced "dee-oh-jay") or clerking for the Supreme Court, and you shouldn't go into a second- or third- or fourth-tier school with the expectation that you will.

And, finally, people who are looking for a highly intellectual or theoretical approach to the law will be disappointed outside the top fifteen. If you want to ponder the monopoly effects of the patent law regime, or write papers about the influence of John Locke on property law, or spend a good chunk of Criminal Law talking about competing theories of deterrence, you're going to have a harder time finding that the further down the food chain you go. Your experience also won't be as interdisciplinary. It won't be routine, for example, for Aristotelian philosophers to be teaching seminars called Theories of Mercy, or for federal judges to guide you through Melville in Law and Literature.

PRICE TAGS

You've all heard of people who get engaged with the thought that they can always back out before the big day, but then they've ordered the invitations and bought the bridesmaids' dresses, and guests have made their travel plans. Somehow the whole thing snowballs and the next thing they know, they're married. The momentum is so strong that people give up a little piece of their free will in the process. Applying to law school is a lot like getting engaged. Once people start down that road, it's hard to keep a clear head. Lots of people who should be backing out of the law school "engagement" don't.

I know how exciting it is—the euphoria and light-headedness of receiving those fat envelopes. You've worked so hard to get here—kicking butt in college and at work, enduring those anesthetizing LSAT classes, spending every waking spare minute on your essays and applications, and riding your recommenders. You deserve a pat on the back, but don't fall for a common trap. You've had blinders on for the past six months, if not the past several years. You've been so focused on one goal—getting into a good law school—that you've started to think, "I'll do anything to make it happen! I'll pay any price, bear any burden, to go to law school!"

But law school comes at a cost—a huge cost—and it's very comfortable and easy to relegate that queasy reality to the fold in your brain labeled "Abstractions & Things to Worry About Later." Three years at a private law school will run you about $100,000 to $150,000 these days, including living expenses. Public schools cost just about as much for people who aren't state residents (you're lucky if they are just $10,000 cheaper per year than private schools), and in-state residents sometimes pay just $5,000 to $10,000 less per year than out-of-state applicants do.

That's a lot of money, any way you slice it. Call me a party pooper, call me a curmudgeon, but you'll thank me later if you pull your head out of the sand now and figure out how you're going to pay for this grand adventure. In a perfect world, you'd think about the finances before you decide to apply—indeed, you might make your decision to apply contingent on the financial analysis—but most of us mere mortals don't work that way, so you owe it to yourself to tackle this subject before you send in your deposit and end up "married" to the wrong school or career.

You need to think of your legal education as an investment, and you should calculate your expected return on that investment. That's why it's so important to think about your career options coming out of various law schools. If you have to pay $1,000 a month in after-tax dollars to cover your student loans, you'd better be sure you will be able to find work at a well-paying law firm after you graduate. If you graduate $100,000 in the hole, don't assume for a second that you can run off and work for a public-interest legal clinic. And until you've paid off that debt, or unless you attend a law school with a generous loan-forgiveness program (more on that later), you won't have the freedom to go sit on a beach and stare at your belly button while you contemplate what you really want to do with your life. Think of it this way: Lots of people rush off to law school on the assumption that a law degree gives them freedom, but you don't really have freedom when you've mortgaged the next ten—or thirty—years of your life. (Law school graduates who join large law firms don't have much trouble repaying their loans on the ten-year payment plan, but most law school graduates don't end up joining the big firms, and many end up extending their loan-repayment schedules to thirty years.)

That's also another reason to know exactly what kind of work and lifestyle you're getting yourself into when you decide you want to go to law school. Most applicants say to themselves, "Yeah, I'll go pay my dues at a firm until I'm out of debt, then I'll figure out what I really want to do," but they don't have any real idea what it's like to work at a high-paying firm (if they're even in the running for a job at a big firm when they graduate), and in my experience, only a minority of big-firm lawyers can reasonably be described as happy. They are a pretty miserable lot, in fact. Five years (or more) of any job will feel like the seventh circle of hell when you're miserable. If you graduate with little debt, you have true freedom: the freedom to say, "Screw this, I'm going to go write a novel," or, "Screw this, I'm going to go start a business," or, "Screw this, I'm going to go stay home with my kids."

Keep in mind that if you do end up financing your law school education with loans, you'll spend the next ten to thirty years paying interest on every pair of shoes, every manicure, and every tub of popcorn you buy during those three years. Be very sober and frugal about your spending decisions if you'll be living on borrowed money.

Public-Interest Law

If public-interest work is appealing to you—and most applicants to the top schools express that desire—you should think long and hard before going deep into debt, even for a top school. About fifty law schools offer loan-repayment assistance programs (LRAP programs) for graduates who go into low-paying public-interest jobs. Those schools love to advertise their LRAP programs, not least because they are such a great marketing tool. Some *states* also offer LRAP programs (Arizona, Florida, Maryland, Minnesota, North Carolina, and Tennessee, for example).

It is very important to get as much information as you can from each school you're applying to about its LRAP program, and the relevant state bar association will be able to provide you with information about state programs. The details really matter. The LRAP programs all have their own formulas and eligibility requirements, and most of them are very draconian. Some of them are so stingy that they're basically unusable and exist in name only. (The best source for comparing different LRAP programs is www.equaljusticeworks.org.) Also, before accepting an offer from a school whose LRAP program you're interested in, speak to the person who administers the program (usually in the financial aid office, sometimes in the career services office) to find out exactly how the eligibility rules work and have them walk you through the math. (Note that once you have an offer in hand, you can start demanding information in a way that you shouldn't when you're still an applicant.) For example, an LRAP program that phases out once your annual salary hits $40,000 is useless if you have $100,000 in debt. And a program that will deem most of your loans not to be "need based" (more on that later), and therefore ineligible for repayment assistance, won't serve you, either. And finally,

don't assume that LRAP programs will cover your undergraduate or other graduate debt.

FINANCIAL AID

According to the Law School Admission Council, the average debt of law school graduates who took out both federal
and private student loans is currently about $80,000. That
translates, give or take (depending on the interest rate and
the repayment period), into a monthly payment of $1,000.
For many law school graduates, their debt payments are either their largest recurring payment every month or the
second-largest after their rent or mortgage payments. And
don't let yourself be too dazzled by the huge salaries that
you read about. Young attorneys at large firms do indeed
earn a lot of money, but they have to, because they have so
much debt to pay off. (Remember that most law school
graduates don't even end up at fancy, large law firms.) Law
school is an investment, and just like any other investment,
you have to project your expected return on that investment. I encourage you to run different income and debt
scenarios through the excellent financial aid calculators at
www.finaid.org, www.nelliemae.com, and www.accessgroup
.org. You'll have a much better idea of what you can and
can't afford.

    You'll most likely already be familiar with Financial Aid
101 from college, but because parents are usually the ones
who deal with college students' financial aid applications,

many law school applicants will have to go through this rite of passage. The process is also a little different for law school than it is for college, so read on even if you've been around this block before.

Most people can't pay for their law school educations out of pocket, and they rely on three sources to make up the shortfall: scholarships, loans, and part-time or summer jobs. The exact amount that you'll have to cough up will vary from school to school, but the bottom line is that you'll end up having to borrow—or your family will have to pay for—the entire cost of tuition and fees and living expenses (the so-called cost of attendance), minus any scholarship funds the school gives you and any money you earn while you're in school.

Scholarships

Scholarships (also called grants) are funds that the school itself gives you free and clear. Think of them as tuition discounts. Scholarships can be need based, meaning they are tied to your demonstrated financial need (in the opinion of the school), or merit based, meaning they are tied to your past achievement and future promise (also in the opinion of the school). Schools might offer both, either, or neither.

The most important thing for you to understand about scholarships is that even schools that say they meet all demonstrated financial need don't generally meet that need with scholarships; they'll still expect you to borrow most of the cost of your education. The math is very simple: Most people don't have the funds to pay $50,000 a year out of pocket, so to some extent every applicant "needs" a 100 percent scholarship. But scholarship funds are limited, so financial aid officers ration their fixed scholarship budgets among many worthy and needy people as equitably as they can. As a practical matter, that means that almost *nobody* is very happy with the amount of scholarship funds he receives, because scholarships only rarely meet anyone's full need. You'll receive your rationed share based on very draconian formulas (more on those below), and you'll be expected to borrow and earn the rest.

So how does that rationing work? The key to the draconian formulas I mentioned is something called the EFC. Memorize that—it's very important. EFC stands for "Expected Family Contribution," bureaucrat-speak for the amount of money you'll be expected to contribute based on your individual financial circumstances. Let me say that again: the amount you are *expected* to contribute, not the amount you and your family can *actually* contribute or are *willing* to contribute. For most people there's a huge gap between the two, and the sooner you understand this little fiction called the EFC, the sooner you'll snap out of your temporary incredulity and rage and return to your Zen-State Happy Place.

There are generally two different formulas law schools use for calculating your EFC: the Federal Methodology and the Institutional Methodology. (Bureaucrats are so good at inventing catchy names, aren't they?) The better you understand these methodologies, the better you'll understand how your EFC is calculated and how much wiggle room, if any, you have to minimize it.

The Federal Methodology is a formula that Congress determines in order to allocate federal funds (as opposed to private funds you receive through your law school), and it serves as the starting point for a law school when it is trying to determine your need for grant purposes. Your EFC is calculated using the Federal Methodology on a form called the Free Application for Federal Student Aid, or FAFSA for short. (You may remember the FAFSA from college.) You can find out more about the Federal Methodology at www .studentaid.ed.gov, and you can calculate very good estimates of your EFC at www.finaid.org and www.salliemae.com. One very strange thing you'll notice: The FAFSA assumes a dollar is worth the same in New York City as in Amite, Louisiana, and doesn't take regional cost of living into account. That's what you get when you're dealing with the feds, I guess.

In determining how much of their own money to give you, many schools refine that EFC calculation by looking at the FAFSA and applying, in addition, a second formula to determine your need. Those second formulas (which can vary from school to school) are referred to as the Institutional Methodology, to distinguish them from the FAFSA's Federal Methodology. For the Institutional Methodology, a school might use special forms that it developed itself, but most schools use the formulas provided by one of two sources: the

Need Access form offered by Access Group, or the PROFILE
form offered by the College Board. (Of the two, most schools
use the PROFILE.) You can find out more about the Need
Access application at www.accessgroup.org and the PRO-
FILE application at www.collegeboard.org.

Note that most public law schools use only the FAFSA,
which offers some real advantages for the following reasons.
Both forms look at your own finances as well as your spouse's
(if you're married). They also take into account, to varying
degrees, how many children you have and how much they're
costing you. The upside to the Federal Methodology is that
it doesn't take your *parents'* finances into account. Because
you're applying to graduate school, you're automatically
considered financially independent from your parents, even
if you still live at home. "Yippee!" you think, but don't get
too excited, because your parents' finances still count for
most versions of the Institutional Methodologies that many
private schools use to allocate their own money.

The two methodologies reward and penalize individual
circumstances differently. For example, the Federal Methodology doesn't count your house as an asset. Institutional
Methodologies, on the other hand, usually do count your
house in calculating your assets, but allow you to protect
some of your income for your family's elementary and high
school expenses and take into account much more information about your medical expenses. However, before you move
assets into someone else's name, spend them down, or try to
game the system in some other way before applying for finan-

cial aid, you should run different scenarios through the online calculators. These allow you to generate very close estimates of your EFC under both formulas (see www.finaid.org).

There are a couple of things you should realize before you make yourself crazy trying to game the system. First, make peace with the fact that you'll feel screwed under both methodologies, no matter what you do, because you'll be expected to use just about all income and assets for your education, and your EFC will seem jaw-droppingly huge either way. Most people aren't willing to wipe out most of their retirement savings, for example, to pay for school, but these formulas assume that you should be cashing in nearly all your assets.

The other assumption of most schools' EFC calculations that makes most people laugh—in despair and incredulity—is the extent to which the parents of grown-ups are expected to help out their kids. Under most Institutional Methodology formulas, they, too, are expected to wipe out many of their assets to send you to graduate school. Funny, huh? You can get indignant about that, and argue till you're blue in the face that your parents, even if they have the means, aren't willing to pay for your law school education, but believe me when I tell you to save your breath. Financial aid officers know how silly that is in certain cases, but that's just one of the ways they ration their limited resources.

Put yourself in their shoes for a second: If they changed their policies and stopped taking parental earnings and assets into consideration, how many parents do you think would admit that they're willing to pay? Pretty close to zero, right? It would create horrible incentives. That doesn't help applicants whose well-off parents really, truly aren't willing to contribute, and they are just out of luck. If it's any consolation, even people who don't have the means still end up with laughably high EFC numbers and have to borrow the difference between what these formulas *say* they can pay and what they really *can* pay. We call that difference "replacement borrowing" (or "gap borrowing"). That's one of the reasons applicants interested in LRAP programs should find out how much of their loans are deemed need based and how much are deemed replacement borrowing, because the latter portion is often not eligible for those programs.

Second, you need to understand that law schools use these formulas only as starting points. Ultimately, the person who is responsible for allocating funds and assessing your need looks at your forms and can decide, in her discretion, whether to revise the bottom line upward or downward. It is a very subjective process, even though all those forms and formulas give the illusion of an objective, standardized analysis.

A third, and closely related, point is that at most law schools, there really is no meaningful distinction anymore between need-based scholarships and merit scholarships. At the end of the day, they are fungible: At most schools, both come out of the same financial aid budget. (At a small minority of schools, financial aid and admissions are completely separate, and the financial aid officers won't know if someone is needy when awarding merit money.) If a school really wants you, it will offer you more money than if it doesn't, so whether it calls the money it offers you a "need-based" or "merit" scholarship is really a cosmetic distinction. (That's another reason not to get your hopes up for a lot of need-based money unless you're a really good catch for a school.) And law schools can actually see a list of the other schools to whom you are submitting your FAFSA, so they can do some modeling and try to project what they might need to offer you if they want to snatch you away from the competition. The bottom line here is that if you think you are very deserving, whether as a matter of need or merit, you should be making your case to admissions officers, not necessarily the financial aid office (which is typically more focused on processing your forms and helping you with your loan applications and the like).

If the process is so discretionary, can you negotiate for a better aid package? If you think you have the leverage because you're such a good catch for a particular school, you can give it a try (be nice about it). Scholarships are basically tuition discounts that schools offer to people they really want. What makes you a good catch for scholarship purposes? Typically, you're a good catch if you have the *numbers* that a school wants in order to keep up their medians for the *U.S. News* rankings, or you are a member of a *demographic group* that the school is courting. Everything else is just icing as far as scholarships are concerned. So if your numbers are average for a particular school, don't expect to get more money just because, for example, you were awarded a Fulbright since you applied. The *U.S. News* rankings don't reward schools for the number of Fulbright Scholars they have, and schools don't really track groups beyond race, sex, and, to a lesser degree, geography.

If you do appeal for more money, you'll help your cause if you can show that a *peer* school offered you more money—you won't get more lovin' if you show that a school lower down the food chain offered you more money. That's just supply and demand. Still, in my experience, very few awards are changed based on other offers. Also, these are nonprofit folks we're talking about here. They are likely to find the notion of a bidding war pretty distasteful, so don't push your luck. They won't retract their offer if they think you're a jerk, but you don't want to alienate people whom you should befriend. On a related note: Do you give up financial aid leverage if you apply binding early decision? Absolutely, because they know that they don't need to woo you away from their competitor schools with money.

Loans

The good news (or better news, anyway) is that it's much easier to borrow for your education as a law school student than as a college student *if you have a good credit history*. The federal government lets U.S. citizens and permanent residents borrow up to $18,500 a year. If, based on the FAFSA, you are deemed to have need, you can borrow up to $8,500 of that total annual $18,500 at subsidized interest rates. In case it's not clear to you, let me emphasize what a great deal that is: While you're in school, the American taxpayer pays the interest on that loan. If you need to borrow more than $8,500, you can borrow up to an additional $10,000 a year at unsubsidized interest rates for a total of up to $18,500 a year. (Note that there is a lifetime limit of $138,500, including your undergraduate and graduate federal loans, but most people don't bump up against it.)

If you still need to borrow above and beyond that $18,500, it is pretty easy to borrow the remainder, up to the total cost of attendance, from private lenders *if you have good credit.* The interest rates and fees are higher (because they're not subsidized by the taxpayer), but you can usually shave a bit off if you have a parent or other qualified borrower co-sign. (To find out what your credit report looks like, you can order it from www.experian.com.) You can compare different private loan offerings at www.estudentloans .com. The law school you end up choosing might also have standing arrangements with particular lenders to facilitate the private lending process for its students, but don't assume they're always the better deal.

If you have a poor credit history, you may have to wait months if not years to clean it up. And note that if you have ever defaulted on a government loan before, for example in college, you may not be eligible for more government loans.

Jobs

Some law school students earn big bucks working for law firms part-time during the school year and full-time during the summers. When you're comparing financial aid offers, find out whether the law school's offer is good for all three years, or whether your aid is adjusted each year. In the latter case, find out whether the school will reduce your aid based on your earnings (some schools reduce aid on a dollar-for-dollar basis).

Tips

1. If you have to fill out the Need Access form or the PROFILE (see page 242), get those out of the way before you complete your FAFSA. The FAFSA will be a breeze when you're done with those.

2. Get your FAFSA and other required forms in as early as possible after January 1. You or your parents might not be ready to file your taxes yet, but you should gather that information as early as possible. Financial aid is awarded on a first-come, first-served basis, and the sooner you get all your forms in, the better for you. This also means that if you're admitted to a law school later in the year (say, you just came off a waitlist), you likely won't have as much access to financial aid funds as people who were accepted earlier in the process. Once the financial aid budget is gone, it's gone.

3. The financial aid process is a family affair. Your parents can make your life very, very difficult, or reasonably easy, because in many cases they will also have to fill out complicated forms and disclose sensitive information for your financial aid applications.

4. Protect your credit rating and credit history. Many applicants, especially ones right out of college, are surprised to find that their credit reports show every utility bill that went unpaid. If you have spotty credit, you must clean it up if you want to have access to federal or private loans. Order your credit report and fix any mistakes as soon as possible.

CHAPTER 9

Final Thoughts

I know I've been hammering home the fact that your numbers typically have to be in the ballpark for any given school, but if it were *just* about numbers, computers would be making admissions decisions. Once you're in the ballpark with your numbers, you have a lot of power to influence which letter you receive. Think about that for a minute. So many applicants resign themselves to the notion that the process is *all* a numbers game, or that the process is random and mysterious. Neither is true. I want to leave you with three thoughts:

First: If you are in that mushy middle, hovering right around a school's medians, *you have almost total control over which letter you receive.* That's a lot of power, and people who underestimate or blow off the "soft" parts of the application throw that power right out the window.

Second: If you're going to apply to law school, *do it right the first time.* Some people take the LSAT or submit a few applications on a lark just to see how they'll do. Other people agonize over every little detail but have no idea what they're doing. Both approaches are terrible ways to spend your time and your money, and turning in half-baked applications can really hurt you down the road. Those people have two choices, neither of them attractive. Either they make peace with their selection of offers and invest their futures in a school that isn't as good as one they could have attended, or they decide they're going to give it another go but have already compromised their reapplication chances, *even if* they do everything right the second time.

And third: *Few decisions have a more profound impact on your future than where you go to school.* So much of what follows—your educational experience, career opportunities, salary potential, geographic flexibility, and alumni networks—hinges on this choice. Are there people who end up defying the odds after graduation? Sure. Do you really want to be fighting the odds? Probably not. Investing some time and effort now to maximize your opportunities will pay for itself a dozen times over down the road. Many employers care more about where you went to school than how you did there, so getting in is often the hardest part. You'll find people crawling out of the woodwork to give you advice on different law schools and your applications, but be a smart consumer and consider your sources.

It's your life. Choose wisely.

APPENDIX A

Brainstorm Questionnaire

ANNA IVEY
Admissions Counseling

BRAINSTORM QUESTIONNAIRE

These brainstorming questions serve three goals. Your answers will allow me to do the following:

1. better understand your background and motivations,

2. better understand your personal "balance sheet": your strengths, your weaknesses, and the best marketing strategy for you, and

3. help us identify good essay topics and improve your résumé.

The best applications are the result of a certain amount of soul-searching and introspection, so please answer these questions carefully and candidly. These answers are not for public consumption, so at this point do not try to spin your answers as if you were writing them for an admissions officer. Remember: I know next to nothing about you, so I'm trying to get a snapshot of you as efficiently as possible.

Please also spend as much time as you can on this brainstorming exercise. There is no page limit, and there's no need to apologize for long answers. The heavy lifting you do now in answering these questions has the greatest potential payoff in terms of the help I can give you.

Full name:

E-mail address:

Best phone number(s) to reach you at:

Fax number (if you have access to a fax machine):

Mailing address:

1. What is your age?

2. Where did you grow up?

3. What do/did your parents do for a living? How would you describe your childhood and young adulthood? What kind of high school did you attend? Were there any unusual circumstances when you were growing up?

4. If not obvious from #2, have you spent significant amounts of time outside the United States?

5. What languages do you know besides English?
   What is your proficiency?
   How did you acquire that proficiency?

6. Are you a demographic minority? Do you plan on self-identifying as such in your applications? Is there anything else about your background that would contribute to the diversity (broadly defined) of a law school class? Examples: you were the first in your family to go to college, you're an immigrant, you grew up in a town of six hundred people, you used to be a fighter pilot, you're forty years old with grown kids, you descend from an ancient Chaldean tribe in Iraq, etc.

7. What is your religious background and level of commitment, if any?

8. Do you play an instrument? If so,
   What instrument?
   For how long?
   What level of proficiency?
   What kind of music/training (e.g., classical, popular, etc.)?

9. Where did you attend college? How did you pick your college? In hindsight, how would you pick differently and why? Ditto for any graduate programs.

10. What was your major? How did you pick your major? In hindsight, how would you pick differently and why? Ditto for any graduate programs.

11. Tell me about your college performance:

What is/was your GPA?
How does your GPA compare to your school's average GPA?
Is your major considered more difficult than others?
When will/did you graduate?
Did you take unusually difficult classes?
Is there a slump in grades that you need to explain?
Did you have an opportunity to write a senior thesis?
If you wrote a senior thesis, what was the topic and length?
If you are or were in a graduate program, how did you do there?

12. Tell me about any honors or awards you won in college. For each one, please tell me:

Its name:
What for:
The selection criteria:
How many people are eligible for it each year, and how many people win it each year:

13. Please tell me about the last four jobs you've held, in reverse chronological order. (Don't cut and paste from your résumé. Pretend you are telling me about your jobs in conversation.)

Dates:
Job title:
Employer name:
What line of work is your employer in generally?
What did your job involve generally?

What were your three most significant responsibilities?
To whom did you report?
Why did you take this job? Did it meet your expectations?
Did you manage people, budgets, or projects? If so, please elaborate.
What were the three most important skills you learned and used?
What are the three accomplishments of which you are most proud?
What aspects of the job did you find most rewarding?
If you don't work at that job anymore, why did you leave?

14. Please list five possible recommenders. (If you've already asked people for recommendations, please indicate that and answer these questions for them only. If you have copies of their letters, please send me copies.) For each one, please list:

Name:
His/her relationship to you:
How closely he/she knows you:
How long he/she has known you:
Which of your qualities he/she will be able to discuss:

(List as many specific experiences and examples as you can that serve as evidence of those qualities. This will help me evaluate the usefulness of the recommendation.)

15. Please tell me about any problems that you might need or want to explain to an admissions committee, like academic probation, run-ins with the law, substance abuse problems, etc. (Your applications— and later on, the state bar you apply to—will ask you about these issues, so it's best for us to discuss them up front.)

16. What are the three most important factors that you need to be happy at work?

17. What are the three most important factors that you need to be happy in school?

18. What do you consider your three biggest disappointments or failures? (Please answer candidly. Avoid answers like, "I don't characterize any negative experiences as failures.") What would you do differently, in hindsight?

19. What do you consider your biggest weakness in your professional or academic life? (Please answer candidly. Avoid answers like, "I'm a perfectionist," or, "I work too hard.") Some examples: being too blunt with people, procrastinating, or poor people skills. What have you done to overcome that weakness?

20. Tell me about the six most meaningful (to you) extracurricular activities, hobbies, or interests, past or present. Examples include sports, community service, journal writing, website design, reading, politics, etc. Please give as much detail as possible—for example, if you list reading, please list typical books, magazines, or newspapers. Also, please list any unusual activities, like competitive ballroom dancing or bonzai tree cultivation.

    Activity:
    Dates:
    Hours per week or year:
    Position, if applicable. Appointed? Elected? By whom?
    If an organization, what is its purpose or mission?
    What are your most important accomplishments?
    What do you find rewarding about that activity?

21. Your career goals are important to many law schools. Please be as specific as possible here.

What are your short- and long-term career goals?
What part of the country or world do you want to end up in?
What research have you done, or what observations have you made, about law school and the practice of law?
Why is this the right time for you to go to law school?

22. Have you applied to law school before? If so,

    When?
    Which schools and what results?

23. What things are most important to you in choosing a law school?

24. What schools do you think you might want to apply to and why?

25. Have you taken the LSAT yet?

    If so, please list all scores as well as the months and years.
    If not, when do you plan on taking it?
    How did you prepare/are you going to prepare for it?

26. Are you working with your college pre-law adviser? If so,

    Who?
    How closely are you working together?
    What advice is he/she giving you?

27. How are you going to pay for law school?

28. If you weren't going to law school, what would you see yourself doing for the next five or so years?

29. Are you at all tempted by other graduate degrees besides law school?

30. Is there anything else you would like to tell me about yourself?

Please also send me:

- ▓ Your official transcripts (photocopies are fine, but please copy both sides)

- ▓ Your résumé, if you have one

- ▓ Your Academic Summary Report (available from your online LSAC account once LSAC has processed your transcripts)

- ▓ Your LSAT Score Report from LSAC once you have taken the LSAT

- ▓ Your previous law school applications, if applicable

APPENDIX B

Sample Essays

Publisher's note: Throughout the appendixes, the reader will find samples of good as well as bad essays, recommendations, résumés, and addenda. Typographical errors and mistakes have been placed intentionally and are meant to illustrate examples of common stumbling blocks where applicants can go wrong.

GOOD PERSONAL STATEMENT—*TATTOO TOM*

Tattoo Tom sat in his wheelchair at the entrance of the Veterans Administration hospital, basking in the California sun, smoking his Marlboro, and greeting visitors that Wednesday afternoon. He was an Alzheimer's patient, and at the sight of me, he didn't waste any time in waving, pointing toward the sky, and telling me he was enjoying the sun. I simply smiled, said hi, and told him I would be back later, on this, my first day as a volunteer at the Alzheimer's and dementia wards. I didn't want to stare, but as I walked into the hospital, I had to turn back to take a second look. He was *entirely* covered in tattoos.

After my three-hour orientation, I felt overwhelmed by the stale and musty smells of the mental hospital and saddened by the sight of the elderly and ill who were unable to participate in the life around them. I temporarily consoled myself by thinking that perhaps they were all in a common world and that I was the odd one out. I was surprised by how uncomfortable being in this situation made me. My volunteer experience with the elderly in high school had not prepared me for dealing with the discomfort of these mentally ill patients. Their fates seemed predestined. I did not even know these patients, and already I had a knot in my throat and stomach. I began to doubt whether I would be able to volunteer here. As I left the building, I turned to Tattoo Tom and said good-bye. He wasn't so friendly this time. "Don't come back. You didn't keep your promise to me. Go home," he said. My heart sank. I had hurt his feelings and deserved to have mine hurt in return.

I was anxious when I arrived the next week. I wondered if I would be as uneasy as I had been last time. Part of me wanted to stay away from Tattoo Tom to protect myself from his rudeness, but the rest of me was ashamed for hurting his feelings and wanted to see him first thing. He still sat there enjoying the sunshine, just like the week before. This time, I took him for a walk in the garden and we began talking about our backgrounds. I did not expect to have a coherent conversation with an Alzheimer's patient, but we did. As soon as Tattoo Tom found out I was originally from Mexico, he told me about his trip there thirty years ago.

We talked about his Naval service in World War II, his family, the weather, and, of course, the terrible food he was served in the hospital. I learned what it was like for him to have a terminally ill mother while being away at war in the Pacific. He had managed by convincing himself that if he were not defending the country, the chances of her making it through would not be any greater. That experience taught him to let go of things over which he had not control. I had underestimated his intellect out of sheer ignorance, assuming that his disease would compromise his abilities.

One afternoon I was helping the nurses distribute dinner trays when a nurse told me Tattoo Tom wanted me to join him at his table for dinner. This was a first. The nurses were equally surprised because he had a reputation for being antisocial at mealtimes. I joined Tattoo Tom as he was about to eat his chicken stew, cooked carrots, and tapioca. He offered to share his meal, and after staring at his plate, he put his fork down, looked at me with teary eyes, and said, "Young lady, you make me feel alive; that and your friendship mean a lot to me." I felt the same way about him and told him so.

I soon realized that the reaction I had had on my first day to the painful reality of the mental health ward had affected Tattoo Tom as well. He was lonely in a hospital ward with forty other patients. He no longer had the ability to build meaningful friendships with his peers and did not have family anywhere nearby. He lived day in and day out seeing other patients pass away, move to the dementia ward, or simply drift off into a world of their own. He couldn't just walk away as I could. He also worried every day about what would happen to him, and if he would even be cognizant. I felt humbled.

On bad days, despite being disoriented, feeling light-headed, and drooling uncontrollably, he did not let his ailments get in the way of his positive outlook on life. Just like when he had been fighting in the War, he was again in a situation he could not control. He often made light of his situation and reminded himself that he could be in a worse position. Tattoo Tom's courage taught me to dig deeper to find that last bit of power that keeps me moving in the right direction when I am frightened about life's uncertainties.

I saw Tattoo Tom every Wednesday except those few when he was so disoriented that he didn't come out of his room. My three years at the ward broadened my perspective about what it means to appreciate life both for its great tragedy and its great beauty. Tattoo Tom was ending his accomplished life in a mental hospital yet still had so much to offer. Putting his life on the line in the Navy had humbled him and kept him from succumbing to the false belief that the world revolved around him. His insight into the brevity of life and into the scale of his own impact on the world came from being in the War. His experience made him focus on contributing to the development and experiences of others and not just on building a legacy of his own.

Tattoo Tom has since passed away. I try to live as he might by balancing my future goals with present opportunities to better the lives of others and appreciate those along the way who help me. The first day I walked into the hospital, I was a twenty-year-old hoping to bring a little happiness and fresh air to these patients, and I had doubted my ability to do even that. I have since realized that on that day I walked into one of my greatest life lessons.

GOOD PERSONAL STATEMENT—*MORRIS 405*

I was mentally worn-out, and I had never felt better. I was standing in Morris 405, my nightly niche in the mathematics building at Covington University. Staring at the board and at the chalk in my hand, I had proven a fascinating phenomenon in elementary number theory: Three can be divided into *any* number whose digits add up to a number divisible by three. Take the number inscribed on the classroom door, 405. Its digits add up to nine (four + zero + five = nine). Since nine is divisible by three, so is 405. Change the ordering of the digits any way you like: 504 or 054, 450 or 540, and the result will be divisible by three, too! Constructing a proof that would apply to any number up to infinity was a time-consuming process of trial and error filled with false starts and dead ends, but I loved the mental challenge. The result was electrifying in its beauty. The proof decorated the entire board with mathematical symbols, each tied together with reason and logic as its glue. And it made a profound statement—indeed, an undisputable truth—about the *whole* field of numbers, numbers that you and I will never encounter in our lives.

As I stared at the finished proof, I noticed music coming in from an office nearby, a familiar melody. Ah! It was Beethoven. But not just any Beethoven, a passage from the second movement of "Eroica," which had been a favorite of mine ever since I first heard it in high school. Like the proof on the board, the sounds emanating into the room were almost intoxicating in their beauty. And like the symbols and statements that filled the board, the notes and passages of "Eroica" embraced one another, each flowing fluently from those that came before it. But "Eroica" had something more to it than the scribbles on the board: It stirred emotions that mathematics never touched, feelings of hope, fear, and desire that were distinctly mine and that only I could understand. For me, that is the true beauty of music. Take any piece you like, Mozart or Debussy, Madonna or Queen, and no two people will ever hear the same story. Then take the proof on the board. It will *always* make the same statement: Three can be divided into *any* number whose digits add up to a number divisible by three. And it will always be true (that is the splendor of logic). To me, that is the fundamental difference between music and mathematics: Enchantingly, mathematics never allows room for individual meaning or interpretation.

The sounds of "Eroica" from the nearby office transported me back to high school, where—as on that evening at Covington U—I passed away many a night in a classroom, detached from the rest of the world. The room was Bulfinch 108, the Cello Studio at the Holst School of the Arts, a boarding performing arts high school in Springfield. Back then, I was being trained to become an elite classical musician, an orchestral cellist. I used my time in Bulfinch 108 to devour the magnificent symphonies of Brahms and Haydn, Mahler and Beethoven. Somehow, I ended up in Morris 405, devouring the great theorems of Euclid and Newton,

Riemann and Fermat. I was doing something fundamentally different than I would have ever imagined in high school. I had crossed an arc from the symphony to the theorem, passion to logical rigor—music to mathematics.

I had known all through high school that I would never make my life in an orchestra; for me, the life of the orchestral cellist seemed too fixed, and too inequitable. The orchestral cellist begins his training at an arts high school, finishes at a conservatory eight years down the road, and spends the rest of his life perfecting twenty-some measures out of Shostakovich no. 1 and Bruckner no. 3, waiting for an orchestra seat to open—for a colleague to die. When that happens, he competes against thousands of other well-qualified cellists for the vacant seat. And if he wins it—a big if—he moves his family across the country and plays the same twenty-five or thirty symphonies year after year; at the top of his profession, he earns one-third the salary of a second-rate plastic surgeon. That said, I loved music, and went off to Birmingham College in New Rochelle, New York, where I took academics and continued to study under Isaac Ma at Juilliard (with whom I studied all through high school). Though I treasured the New York music scene, the academic scene at Birmingham College left much to be desired, and so I came to Covington U. I had never taken mathematics seriously; once at Covington U, I placed into basic trigonometry, which I simply took to meet a collegewide requirement. The class turned out to be a fun, engrossing intellectual puzzle: I spent one month on one aspect of trigonometry, the next month on another, a week here and a week there. By the end of the term, I put it all into a mentally coherent piece so that if I knew one piece of the puzzle, I could easily derive the rest. It involved little memorization, and a lot of understanding. I absolutely loved it, and that is how I ended up in Morris 405.

Lest I give you the wrong impression, my nights have not always been so scholastic and romantic. Before Morris 405 and Bulfinch 108 (and for a whole year after high school), I spent my evenings working at the Golden Nugget Diner in Mobile, Alabama. My family had immigrated to Mobile from Bangladesh when I was ten years old. My parents, both full-time cooks at the diner, persuaded the owner to hire me as a dishwasher very early on—sixth grade, in fact.

I despised working at the restaurant (alongside my two parents, to boot!). But, in hindsight, working at the Golden Nugget was one of the best things that ever happened to me. Once my English improved—I came to the United States without having ever spoken a word of English—the owner moved me to the front of the restaurant to "run" the cash register (where, among other things, I calculated totals faster than the register, impressing the patrons). Working at the register, I spoke to people with whom I normally had no contact: doctors, teachers, lawyers, and bankers—all of them customers. A young mathematician at heart, I "reduced" all of the customers to a "lowest common denominator" and realized that most of them had one characteristic in common: education. Similarly, when I "reduced" all the employees in the kitchen in a similar fashion, I discovered that none of them had ever gone to college; indeed, many, like my parents, had not even finished high school. Sooner or later, I began to envy the customers who seemed to lead better lives, lives in which people were able to enjoy a night off dining out with family and friends. I did not want to spend the rest of my life like my parents, toiling away hour after hour in a kitchen, unaware, as my mother has routinely been in the past, of the instrument that I played in performing arts high school, or even my major at Covington U. And so I vowed to get an education. What getting an education involved, I had no clue. Whatever it was, it would be my ticket to becoming one of the customers. The evidence was right there, sitting in front of me night after night, in the many booths and tables of the Golden Nugget. Today, many years later, when I go to a restaurant to eat, the erratic clashes of the dishes coming from the kitchen, much like the sounds of "Eroica" coming into Morris 405, remind me that I have followed another arc: I have moved from one side of the register to the other.

I have made many journeys so far: from Bangladesh to America, from the register to the table, from music to math. But my journeys are not yet complete. Just as I complete my passage from the symphony to the theorem, I begin a new one from the theorem to the contract, from college to law school. The outcome, like many times before, could be anything: I may become a public defender, a corporate litigator, an immigration attorney, or even a judge. What I do know is that I will continue to bridge different disciplines and discover new passions, just like in my math and music days.

GOOD PERSONAL STATEMENT—
PRETTY HORSES

In the summer of 2001, between the two years of my master's program, I traveled to Fortaleza, Brazil, to practice my Portuguese and to catch up on my reading. Although graduate school had provided me with the opportunity to read a surfeit of books, few had been the kind of reading I really craved: novels. I had not originally planned to go to Brazil for the summer, but the job market was horrible; I realized that it would be cheaper for me to spend the summer in Fortaleza, where my hotel cost only $16 a night, than to rack up debt as an unpaid intern in Washington, D.C. The bad job market turned out to be a blessing, as nothing could have been more fulfilling than this opportunity to spend my summer days reading on a beautiful beach—in a perfect equatorial climate—and my evenings chatting with Brazilians at local cafés and restaurants.

When I left for Brazil, I had just finished the book *All the Pretty Horses*, by Cormac McCarthy, which I thoroughly enjoyed. I was particularly looking forward to the two remaining books in that trilogy, *The Crossing* and *Cities of the Plain*, which were in my bag with my thirty-five other books. Upon boarding the plane to Brazil, I was delighted to discover that the movie on my flight would be *All the Pretty Horses*. After viewing the film, however, I was no longer delighted; the movie was melodramatic, poorly acted, and overwrought. The movie was so horrendous, in fact, that I decided to read something else and save the sequels for later in my trip. Hoping to purge myself of the memory of the movie, I settled into my seat with Philip Roth's *The Dying Animal.*

Fortaleza turned out to be an ideal setting for my summer literary expedition. Having gotten my feet on the ground, I soon adopted a comfortable daily routine that consisted of reading *O Globo,* a Brazilian newspaper, every morning at a friendly, nearby coffee shop (*my* coffee shop) while drinking a *cafezino* (a strong Brazilian coffee) and eating *Pão de Queijo* (Brazilian cheese bread). Later I would walk for several miles along the crowded urban beach, Praia de Iracema, past the modest hotels and the more affluent apartments. I was always overwhelmed by the constant bustle of activity around me and the ever-present *forro,* the somewhat irritating local music prominently featuring the accordion. At the far end of Iracema, I would hail a cab and continue on to one of the quieter beaches farther south.

Over the next six weeks, I read, among others, *Couples* by John Updike; *The Information* by Martin Amis; *East of Eden* by John Steinbeck; *Autobiography of Red* by Anne Carson; *The New York Trilogy* by Paul Auster; *All the King's Men* by Robert Penn Warren; *The Sheltering Sky* by Paul Bowles; *My Ántonia* by Willa Cather; and *The Ground Beneath Her Feet* by Salman Rushdie. I read Saul Bellow while lying in a hammock in a small beach town five hours north of Fortaleza; I read Graham Greene while sitting in a gritty café downtown; and I read Ian Kershaw's biography of

Hitler, a rare nonfiction selection, while lounging in my hotel room, because it was a hardcover and too heavy to carry to the beach.

I was often surprised by my reaction to the books that I read that summer. It struck me that although I loved Cather's beautiful prose and dreamlike descriptions of rural Nebraska, I was disturbed by the unnatural asexuality of her main character. I also found that I was drawn to books with deeply flawed or unlikable protagonists, like Amis's bitter and jealous writer in *The Information,* or Bowles's insufferable couple in *The Sheltering Sky.* There were books—some even by my favorite writers—that I disliked: Philip Roth's *Our Gang,* for example, an unfortunate satire of the Nixon administration written before Watergate; and Updike's *Couples,* which had more appeal as American social history than as literature. There was only one book that I did not care for at all: Faulkner's *The Sound and the Fury,* because his prose was far more difficult for me to comprehend than Portuguese.

Of all the books I read that summer, one rose above the others. That book was *Ada, or Ardor* by Vladimir Nabokov. I had read *Lolita, Pale Fire,* and *Pnin,* but none of these other books had prepared me for the complexity of this one. It was extremely difficult and enigmatic, dealing with issues of philosophy, physics, and love. While the plot of *Ada* is compelling, it is the combination of Nabokov's fluid prose that exploits the full breadth of the English language, his stunning imagery, the story's puzzle-like structure and charged eroticism that makes this novel wholly unique in my mind. I did not understand all of *Ada, or Ardor*, but like many works of art it is powerfully evocative while remaining somewhat impenetrable. It is a book that I know I will return to several more times in my life.

Halfway through my plane flight back to the United States, I finished *Moby Dick*. There were only two more books left in my bag, Cormac McCarthy's *The Crossing* and *Cities of the Plain*, which to this day remain unread. They rest now on my bookshelf, their pristine spines a lasting testament to the power of film.

BAD PERSONAL STATEMENT—*JORGE*

"Those who produce should have, but we know that those who
produce the most—that is, those who work hardest, and at the
most difficult and most menial tasks, have the least."

—Eugene V. Debs

I can still remember when my weekly allowance was the
be-all, end-all of my existence. I would spend the week
hatching schemes and plans about how to spend my Friday
windfall. Would I get a new computer game? A couple of
CDs or DVDs? Or would I pool my money with my friends
for a weekend trip to the beach? One thing was always the
same, though...I was always thinking only of myself.

But Friday was also the day that Jorge would come to
trim our hedges and mow our lawn. It never occurred to me
on those countless Fridays to think about what life must be
like for Jorge. Just I was heading of to the mall or the beach,
Jorge was slaving away in the hot sun, straining behind
a hungry mower or lugging a massive leaf blower. And it
did not strike me as ironic until much later that when I
was younger, mowing the lawn was what I did to earn my
allowance.

I spend a lot of time thinking about Jorge these days,
about the injustice and unfairness of it all. Am I so much
better than Jorge that I deserve to grow up in a comfortable
home with a manicured lawn, while he slaves away his days
making barely enough to feed his family? And if it's not fair

(and I believe it's not!) then who or what can make a difference? Who or what can rectify the inequities inherent in our system?

Lawyers, that's who. I have known since I was a young boy that I wanted to go to law school and become an attorney. But it wasn't until I got to college and learned about the complex interplay of poverty, race, and social justice that I understood why I needed to go. It wasn't until I understood the incredible advantage of my privileged upbringing (and, conversely, the insurmountable obstacle of Jorge's impoverished upbringing) that I understood why I am obligated to go.

Mark Twain once said, "from those to whom much is given, much is expected." And because I have been given so much, I feel it is my duty to fulfill society's high expectations by using the law to right the social wrongs that are tearing our nation apart. Poverty and violence wreck our inner cities, minorities constitute an overwhelming majority of inmates on death row, and the U.S. war on drugs has taken its casualties disproportionately from the ranks of the poor and nonwhite. I want to help change that. I need to help change that. Indeed, I feel duty-bound to dedicate my life to making the world a better place.

BAD PERSONAL STATEMENT—*KOREA*

My parents immigrated to the United States the year before I was born, dreaming of a batter life and hoping that my siblings and I could have more opportunities than they had themselves. And so I grew up as the child of Korean immigrants in a small town in Kansas, where I had trouble with the barriers presented by a different culture and language from what I had been raised with in my family's home. I wasn't like the other children at school in Kansas, and they never let me forget it.

But it was precisely this difference between my ethnic heritage and the culture of the country where I was born that led me to the study of the history of Korea and the Pacific Rim. Still charged with the memories of the clash of cultures from my childhood, I have designed my college curriculum to challenge the existing dialectic and engage in a new relativized discourse.

While at Winchester College, I served for two years as president of the Korean American Student Association. I was hired as a resident adviser for the international students dormitory, where I earned the distinction of RA of the Year. During my junior year, I received honors for the most outstanding paper written in the history department. I took at least two graduate courses during each semester of my junior and senior years, receiving a grade of A– or better in each of them. I served as research assistant for three professors in the history department during my senior year, and contributed research to two scholarly books and four journal articles published in the *American Historical Review*. I was able to present my own work on the history of Korean immigration at the 2002 New England Conference on History and Culture.

During 2003, I received the Winchester College Racial Diversity Fellowship, the Johnson Pre-Dissertation Fellowship, a Gates Millennium Scholarship, a Pew Scholarship, and a scholarship from the Center on Interracial Justice and Equal Rights. I have also been involved for several years in the Inner City Racial Justice Program (ICRJP) and as an academic tutor for a local inner-city high school. I was recognized by ICRJP as Volunteer of the Year.

I hope to continue my work on the history of these peoples and their immigrant experience and feel that immigration law and the laws of citizenship will play an important role. That is why I want to go to law school, and if allowed to attend this august institution, I will endeavor to continue my work in and through the academy of the law.

GOOD STATEMENT OF PURPOSE—
HEALTH LAW

While working as a researcher at California University Hospital, the project I spent the most time on—and the work I was most passionate about—was the development of a novel diagnostic tool for Alzheimer's disease. Previously, no one had been able to positively diagnose Alzheimer's disease without analyzing postmortem tissue (i.e., the patient had to be dead). The work was cutting edge and redefined how the scientific community has since approached Alzheimer's disease research.

With our discovery in hand, we needed to convince the scientific community that our findings were valid and begin the long process of bringing our new diagnostic tool to real patients in real clinics. And so the endless meetings began. How do we present our work so that people receive proper legal credit for their efforts? How could the work be protected so that no one else could claim improper intellectual ownership? Who should own the patent? What companies should we be soliciting to develop the drug? Who owns shares in what company such that the discovery could present a conflict of interest?

Our business and legal meetings, so far removed from the actual science and real patients, discouraged us. My boss went searching for a lawyer who could help us navigate and facilitate the process, and the search was not an easy one. What my boss found was a scarcity of lawyers who have the necessary science background to understand our discovery. I don't think anyone is served when medical innovations are needlessly trapped in the patent process or entangled in never-ending intellectual property disputes. I have watched with sadness as many promising ideas ossify in the basic research stage rather than moving to the clinics, where these innovations could help patients.

I have spent the past five years of my life dedicated to re-searching innovative therapies for people struggling with neurodegenerative diseases like Alzheimer's disease and Lou Gehrig's disease. I have worked under the direction of a Nobel laureate, been published in leading medical journals like *Biochemistry*, and earned a certificate in postbaccalau-reate pre-medical studies to deepen my science and research skills. The biomedical arena is exploding with important therapies, and I want to combine my strong scientific back-ground with a law degree to assist researchers through the complicated legal and regulatory maze that ultimately de-termines whether cutting-edge medical discoveries make their way to doctors and patients. My law degree can take me in several different directions—I might serve as a patent prosecutor or a patent litigator, or as a liaison with regula-tory bodies like the FDA, for example—and I am excited to explore those opportunities further in law school.

Pontchartrain Law School is my first choice. A good friend, Joe Cocoros, graduated from your program last year, and my conversations with him persuaded me that no other law school offers more classes in health-care and medical technology law (classes like "Food and Drug Law" and "Medicine and the Law"). I am also excited about the opportunity to take classes at the Bradley Whitford School of Management and to work at the Sharfman Health Law Clinic. No other law school can offer me access to faculty like Michelle Davies and Ross Boardman, with whom I hope to work. In short, no other law school is a better fit for me and for my career goals, and I am excited about the possibility of joining your community of scholars.

GOOD STATEMENT OF PURPOSE—
COAST GUARD

The message crackled across the encrypted radio on Christmas morning: a three-hundred-foot Panamanian-flagged coastal freighter had been hijacked off the coast of Haiti and was steaming toward Puerto Rico. Imprisoned in his cabin, the Dominican master had placed a desperate cell-phone call and reported that four Cuban hijackers attempting to seek political asylum in the United States had commandeered his ship, stabbing a Bahamian crew member in the process. Haitian authorities had alerted the U.S. Coast Guard, and a reconnaissance aircraft and cutter had been diverted to intercept the ship.

In my seven years at sea, I have taken part in hundreds of law enforcement cases as both a Coast Guard Law Enforcement Officer as well as a tactical commander. Most legal issues I had faced up to that point revolved around the standard fare of lawmen everywhere: Fourth Amendment searches and cut-and-dried immigration issues. Certainly nothing in my tenure as Commanding Officer of a Coast Guard vessel had prepared me for the volatile legal cocktail of extraterritorial jurisdiction, political standing, and international crime I now faced. When I reported aboard, my predecessor had referred to the Greater Antilles Section (GANTSEC) area of operations as the "Wild West." Spanning the entire Caribbean Basin from Haiti to the Lesser Antilles and the north coast of South America, the area is a geographically and culturally divergent haven for smugglers and fugitives who thrive in the no-man's-land created by thirty-two nations and their sovereign but porous borders. The U.S. Coast Guard is the premier law enforcement entity throughout the region, and projects an unparalleled degree of hegemonic authority absent in other geographic areas in which the service operates.

The mission to interdict the freighter and effect a peaceful resolution was clear, the means to such an end, less so. One hundred miles outside of U.S. territorial waters, the ominous radar blip signaled that we were closing in on the hijacked craft. I issued the order to sound General Quarters, the shrill Klaxon summoning the cutter's eighteen crew members to their battle stations. Gunners manned the 25 mm cannon and the .50 caliber machine guns. Tensions mounted.

As the cutter raced abreast of the freighter, the radioman hailed the hijacked craft. After a lengthy pause, a hesitant voice answered the hail, claiming to be the master. As the questioning proceeded, it was apparent that the master was holding his radio's transmit key down, allowing the background conversation to bleed onto the airwaves. Attempting to avert suspicion, the hijackers directed the master to answer questions innocuously. Playing along, I asked for permission to conduct a consensual boarding in order to confirm the vessel's registry and documentation. I gambled that the hijackers would risk a routine consensual boarding (perhaps choosing to hide the hostages) rather than raise further suspicion by refusing. Once the boarding team was onboard, I knew that any evidence of a crime would justify further investigation, regardless of the initial reason for their presence.

As we made preparations to launch our deployable intercept boat, I gathered the boarding team to go over the plan one last time. During the briefing, I was deeply cognizant of the fact that I, as Commanding Officer, was inescapably responsible for whatever befell my crew. After the briefing, I took a step back and surveyed my boarding team: young men (teenagers in some cases) from disparate socioeconomic and ethnic backgrounds, each ready to give his life or take the life of another. All were well trained and experienced, but none had been involved in a case with such enormous implications. Remarkably, even under such incredible pressure, the team exhibited the kind of confident, low-key levity that is peculiar to sailors who have complete faith in themselves, their training, and each other.

This case ended anticlimactically, as many big cases do: The captors mustered with their hostages and were quickly subdued and detained by the boarding team. The crew was treated and allowed to continue the journey while the hostage takers were secured. Because of a lack of nexus to the United States, the State Department chose not to prosecute, pushing instead for one of the other nations involved to prosecute the hijackers. In the end, only Cuba would take them, but diplomatic considerations would not allow for cooperation on the criminal level; the hijackers were repatriated the following week with nothing in the way of a handoff between the two nations.

Incidents like this one are at the heart of my decision to pursue a career in the law. I have spent nearly a decade on the front line of a wide range of legal issues, from search and seizure to international jurisdiction, from criminal law to immigration law. My experiences have left me both well prepared and highly motivated to tackle these and other legal issues as a law student and eventually a practitioner.

Sample Recommendations

GOOD ACADEMIC RECOMMENDATION—
MADELEINE

Dear Sir or Madam:

During my twenty years of teaching American literature at this university, I have rarely looked forward to entering a classroom more than when Madeleine Shaw was sitting in the front row, alive with anticipation and having meticulously dissected the reading assignment. Quite frankly, she was the only student in my introductory American Gothic Literature class who was better versed in Edgar Allan Poe than I. While not flaunting this fact (which astute fellow students picked up on in no time anyway), she nonetheless relished the academic sport of lively repartee and intellectual exchange. Other students in the class were riveted as Madeleine single-handedly turned a course that otherwise could have threatened—on paper at least—to be a ho-hum freshman curricular mandate into an adventure that left all of us anticipating what the ninety minutes would hold in store each time. Students who considered themselves unforgivingly "analytical" began to revel in what one freshman described as "using the other side of my brain—thanks to Madeleine."

Madeleine showed the rest of the class that iambic pentameter is more than a mathematical exercise. Although I flattered myself in thinking that my occasional role was that of a muse—to turn some young minds on to the beauty of American literature—it was Madeleine who infected her contemporaries, and soon all were coming to class as extraordinarily well prepared as she. Without a hint of hubris, this gifted young mind had an insatiable desire to share her boundless joy of the written word and so opened up worlds that might otherwise have drowned in the prosaic.

Madeleine's essay on the poem "Annabel Lee" received the only A+ I have given in two decades of teaching. There has been a bell curve of A's in my academic career, but only one student ever deserved an A+. When I asked her to read the poem aloud, she received a standing ovation, and this from students who knew she was adversely affecting the grading curve and ultimately their own GPAs. She has this effect on her peers. And she certainly left an indelible mark on me. Although I am hardly an expert on the law, I suspect that the legal world might not be ready for Madeleine in a courtroom.

It has been three years since Madeleine enrolled in my course, and we have stayed in contact throughout her undergraduate years. The poetry readings she started in her freshman dormitory now enjoy the largest and most faithful following among the university's extracurricular offerings. By popular demand, the evenings are scheduled so as not to coincide with Dungeons and Dragons campaigns, of which she is also an active and formidable participant. She will be sorely missed by this university, and my colleagues regret only that we do not have a law school where we could continue to watch her dazzle everyone around her.

BAD ACADEMIC RECOMMENDATION—*LOUIE*

Dear Sir or Madam:

It is with great pleasure I commend to you Louie Bransford. Louie has majored in pre-law during his four years at our institution, and I have known him during this, his senior year. He writes well, which obviously is an indispensable asset for anyone going into law. His German to English translations are almost always above average in quality. On at least two occasions, we have also met outside the classroom, and I find him to be well-spoken and articulate.

To fulfill his foreign language requirement at our university, Louie enrolled in my German II class. It was gratifying to see that he could grasp different parts of speech and understand cases, and because of this talent, he received a solid "B" in my class. It is unfortunate that he did not attend our field trip to a local "Oktoberfest" because he had other plans, but perhaps he will find other venues to improve his spoken German.

Louie is an amiable student with an upbeat attitude, and he is well liked by students and faculty alike. He is looking forward to graduation and the next chapter of his life. He genuinely aspires to improve the public image of lawyers, and I think he will do so.

GOOD PROFESSIONAL RECOMMENDATION—
SARA

Dear Sir or Madam:

For the past six months, Sara Velasquez has been working part-time at our law firm as a file clerk to help finance her last year in college. Our firm has employed dozens of students in this capacity for more than eleven years (all from local schools like Harvard, BU, BC, and Northeastern), but none has impressed me more, or made more of an impact on our firm, than Sara.

From day one I could tell that Sara was different: She was energetic, enthusiastic, attentive, and inquisitive far beyond the level of a normal part-time file clerk. She showed up at the office with a small spiral notebook, which she used to jot down office procedures, tips from co-workers, and even various rules of civil procedure as they became relevant to whatever task was at hand. We were all amazed at her ability to move rapidly up the rather steep learning curve of our varied and complicated practice (we handle everything from criminal defense work and family law to collections and contract disputes). Within the first week, Sara achieved a 90 percent recognition rate on the names and details of the various plaintiffs, defendants, and other parties involved in our considerable caseload.

Sara is not just bright and inquisitive, she is also meticulous and thorough. She oversees the docket calendar, often taking the initiative to file the necessary continuances in various courts in the Commonwealth (many courts have their own idiosyncrasies), while ensuring that opposing counsel assent to the calendar change as well. Sara has also mastered the art of searching online records such as those on file with the Secretary of State. She has gotten to know many of the county sheriffs by name, an incredibly shrewd practice that enables her easily to verify whether a defendant has been served appropriately and in a timely manner. All this from a student we originally hired as a file clerk!

Some weeks after she started working for us, I was surprised to learn that English is not Sara's first language. We knew she was bilingual, but her English was so flawless that we all just assumed that she had studied Spanish in school. Unlike some of our other students for whom English was a second language, Sara communicates in utterly natural English, never hesitating to pick up the phone and call a clerk or magistrate to inquire about a particular case. Indeed, her ability to speak both Spanish and English with native fluency has proven to be one of her most valuable assets. We often use Sara to communicate with Spanish-speaking defendants and their attorneys, and on more than one occasion, Sara actually helped negotiate settlement agreements that resolved the matter at hand without the need for further litigation.

On top of all this, Sara is a genuine "people person" who interacts exceptionally well with the other office employees. We all like and respect her very much. Indeed, we will be sorry to see her go when it comes time for her to graduate.

However, we are glad to hear that she has chosen to pursue a career in the law, and I have no doubt that she will reach whatever height to which she aspires.

In short, within an amazingly brief time span, Sara, an invaluable "self-starter," has proven herself to be an indispensable asset to our law firm, indeed the best student who has ever worked with us. I will look forward to watching her legal career unfold; no doubt it will be spectacular.

BAD PROFESSIONAL RECOMMENDATION—
JENNIFER

Dear Sir or Madam:

Jennifer Laughton came to our law firm as a paralegal approximately one year ago and joined our real estate group. We hired her right out of college and have been very pleased with her writing and research skills. Jennifer is bright, hardworking, and collegial. When we assign work to her, we are always confident that she will do an excellent job. She is one of the best paralegals I have worked with. She also has a wonderful sense of humor, and we love having her around. She also does a wonderful job organizing our annual trivia contest.

Through our firm, Jennifer has seen a broad spectrum of legal practice and is undaunted by it. She has from time to time taken on assignments in our tax, litigation, and corporate groups. She believes that she can be more than a paralegal and for this reason wishes to attend law school. Based on my experience as a practicing attorney, she undoubtedly will succeed in law school and the practice of law as she has in her role of paralegal, and we wish her all the best.

Sample Résumés

DAT NGUYEN—BEFORE

DAT NGUYEN
158 11th Ave. ❖ Brunswick, ME 04011 ❖ (207) 555-1111

Bowdoin College, Brunswick, ME
  Bachelor's Degree in English, May 2005
  Minor in Film Studies

Honors:
  High Honors
  Dean's List
  Sigma Tau Delta International English Honor Society
  James Bowdoin Scholar

Points of Interest:
  "The Configuration of Bodies in the *Alien* Films"
  "Intertextuality in Dan Simmons's *Hyperion*"
  "Cyberspace and the Real World in William Gibson's *Neuromancer*"
  "Under His Thumb: Petruchio, Power, and Patriarchy in *The Taming of the Shrew*"
  "Action Figures: The Evolution of the Modern Action Film, 1962–2003"
  "Pulp Fictions: Masculinity, Race, and Sexuality in the Films of Quentin Tarantino"

Activities:
  Film Club
  Bowdoin Literary Society
  Green Club
  MO3

Things I Do for Fun
  I spend a lot of time perusing my massive DVD, laser disc, and video
  collection. I read an average of about three to four books a week. I
  spend a couple of hours each day corresponding with various persons
  involved in the film and television industry, including Roger Ebert, Rich
  Elias, David Gerrold, and Roger Avary. Also, I read a large number of
  periodicals covering topics ranging from current events to entertainment
  to literary criticism. And, of course, I play video games obsessively.

DAT NGUYEN—AFTER

Dat Nguyen   158 11th Ave., Brunswick, ME 04011

207.555.1111   dat@bowdoin.edu

Experience

Borders Books & Music

2001–Present. Special Orders Clerk.   Portland, ME

- Manage inventory, returns, and special orders for large bookstore with 45 employees and 15,000 sq ft.
- Hired as bookseller, promoted to Special Orders Clerk after only 6 months (2 yrs is average).
- Studying every aspect of running a low-margin, high-volume retail business that must compete with online and catalog-based competition.

Crossroads Medical Associates

1997–2001. Office Manager.   New Wickfield, KS

- Ran day-to-day operations for an office of 2 doctors with a roster of 120 patients.
- Gained firsthand knowledge of the challenges doctors face with respect to tort law, insurance law, Medicare, and workers' compensation.
- Honed ability to work well with superiors, think quickly on my feet, multitask, and meet hard deadlines.

Education

Bowdoin College   Brunswick, ME

B.A. in English expected May 2005.

- Minor in film studies.
- Overall GPA: 3.36 – GPA in Major: 3.8; Dean's List every semester.
- James Bowdoin Scholar (awarded to top 20% of class and requires an honors thesis).
- Senior thesis: "Under His Thumb: Petruchio, Power, and Patriarchy in *The Taming of the Shrew*" (on the underlying misogyny of the Shakespeare classic).

College Activities

Bowdoin College Film Club
2002–Present. Chair, Selection Committee (6 hrs/week).
- Organize weekly showings of classic movies and discussion groups.
- Oversee annual Bowdoin College Film Festival with attendance of 2,000 and a celebrity panel that most recently featured Kevin Smith, Charles Kaufman, and Robert Rodriguez.

MO3
2001–Present. Cofounder (4 hrs/week).
- Cofounded philanthropic/fraternal organization consisting entirely of students writing senior theses.
- Raised $40,000 for the United Way with wildly successful "Casino Night." Recruited professors as casino dealers and organized prize auction.

Publications

- "The Configuration of Bodies in the *Alien* Films," *Lake Brantley Journal of Film*, Fall 2004 (analyzing the use of negative feminine space and misogynist images in films with an ostensibly feminist heroine).
- "Intertextuality in Dan Simmons's *Hyperion*," Locus Magazine Online, LocusMag.com, February 26, 2004 (arguing that a complete reading of Simmons's work is impossible without deep engagement with other texts).
- "Cyberspace and the Real World in William Gibson's *Neuromancer*," Locus Magazine Online, LocusMag.com, December 24, 2003 (examining how Gibson paints a future in which the real seems fantastic and the fantastic seems real).
- "Action Figures: The Evolution of the Modern Action Film, 1962–2003," FilmComment.org, July 2003 (examining the various types of heroes and how they reflected the social and political tenor of their times).
- "Pulp Fictions: Masculinity, Race, and Sexuality in the Films of Quentin Tarantino," *Midwest Journal of Popular Culture*, Winter 2002 (focusing on the intersection of misogyny and racism in Tarantino's 1970s America).

Personal

- Teaching myself to speak Portuguese; saving money for a planned trek through Nepal.

Shelley Fontenot

Second Floor Flat, 40 Turlington Crescent   shelley@wpartners.com
London, W9 1EL, United Kingdom   Tel: (44) (0) 77 99 674 317

EXPERIENCE

12/00–Present   **WPARTNERS (VENTURE CAPITAL)**   London, UK
Associate. Wpartners is a $1 billion fund specializing in early stage technology companies.
- Perform ongoing analysis of portfolio companies and their sectors; serve as liaison with portfolio company management and Wall Street analysts.
- Screen all new business plans and make recommendations to partners; communicate screening decisions to entrepreneurs; communicate key information to investors on a quarterly basis.

01/00–11/00   **DEUTSCHE BANK AG (MERGERS & ACQUISITIONS)**
            London, UK
Associate. Modeled and evaluated multinational mergers using country-specific accounting standards. Trained and mentored new analysts. Executed advisory assignments, including:
- Massive Group plc's $2 billion share offer for ConHugeCo.
- OAG, Bobco, and Rich Capital Partners' $2 billion cash offer for XYZ, Inc.
- Fancy-Pants plc's $336 million sale to Stale Buffalo plc.
- Big-time Holdings Ltd's $100 million sale to Lake Brantley Capital.

06/97–12/99   **DEUTSCHE BANK AG (CORPORATE FINANCE)**
            London, UK
Analyst. Executed lead-managed senior debt financings, including:
- $275 million senior debt for Flintstone Industries, Inc.
- $150 million senior bank facility for Futurama International, Inc.

09/96–05/97   **GOLDMAN SACHS**   New York, NY
IT Intern. Customized software applications for the e-commerce innovations of one of the world's leading investment banking, securities, and investment management firms. Programming languages included C++, PERL, and Java.

EDUCATION

1993–1997 **THE UNIVERSITY OF CHICAGO** Chicago, IL
- B.A. in Mathematics with substantial course work in computer science
- Classes included Financial Accounting at the University of Chicago's Graduate School of Business
- GPA 3.6–3.8 during last 2 years
- Activities:
  - Captain, University of Chicago Math Team. Made team as sophomore (very rare); led team to national championship as junior.
  - Ran the Chicago marathon my junior and senior years.

CERTIFICATIONS

2002 **CHARTERED FINANCIAL ANALYST** London, UK
- Passed Levels I, II, and III at first attempt (19% pass rate).

ACTIVITIES

1997–Present **LONDON EPILEPSY CENTER** London, UK
Epilepsy Sitter. Provide companionship to severe epilepsy patients through weekly 4-hour visits.

1993–Present **STAND-UP COMEDY** Various Locations
Professional Comedian. Act centers on growing up poor and female in the trailers of the U.S. Gulf South.

PERSONAL
- Fluent in French. Reading knowledge of German.
- Enjoy political biographies and French New Wave films (especially Truffaut).

Jake Smith   1422 Third Street, Los Gatos, CA 95030
                                  (408) 555-8700   jakesm@fonapse.com

Experience

ConHugeCo

03/01–Present. Senior Paralegal, Legal Department.   San Jose, CA
ConHugeCo is a multinational hardware company with headquarters in
San Jose.

- Manage a staff of 12 paralegals and case assistants in a
  department with 25 attorneys.
- Exercise budget authority for paralegal staff. Cut costs 24% in my
  first year.
- Doubled productivity over 2 years by creating new tracking and
  monitoring procedures.

Wilson Sonsini Goodrich & Rosati

07/99–02/01. Paralegal, Commercial Litigation Group.   Palo Alto, CA
Wilson Sonsini is one of the country's leading law firms serving a
technology-heavy client base.

- Managed team of 4 temporary paralegals and 3 case assistants.
- Reviewed nearly 1 million pages of documents, on 3 cases, with
  12 attorneys.
- Created reports, charts, and electronic databases tracking
  progression of key issues, events and deadlines.

Self-employed

06/98–07/99. eBay Star Seller.   Los Angeles, CA

- Achieved the highest rating for a seller on eBay, with at least 500
  successful transactions.
- Generated average profits of $3,000 per month while pursuing
  acting career.

Education

Santa Clara University   Santa Clara, CA
B.A. in History, May 1998.

- Overall GPA: 3.67 – GPA in Major: 3.95
- Graduated with honors (awarded to top 10% of class and requires
  honors thesis).

- Honors thesis: "The Salem Witchcraft Trials as Class Warfare: An Econometric Analysis."

Activities

East Palo Alto Legal Aid Project   Palo Alto, CA
11/99–Present. Volunteer Paralegal at organization that provides free legal services to the low-income, largely Latino community of East Palo Alto (6 hrs/wk).

- Typical clients range from battered spouses to criminal defendants to overwhelmed debtors.
- Observed the interplay of race, crime, and immigration in an impoverished community located in the heart of one of the wealthiest and most successful regions in America.

Santa Clara University International Affairs Forum   Santa Clara, CA
10/95–06/96. Chairman (4 hrs/week).

- Organized annual forum with discussion panels featuring international leaders such as Václav Havel, Tony Blair, and Vladimir Putin.
- Organized $25,000 fund-raising campaign to bring in top-notch speakers and publish forum journal.
- Oversaw 300% increase in membership.

San Jose Civil War Reenactment Society   San Jose, CA
11/96–06/97. Membership Director (2 hrs/week).

- Organized annual reenactment of various Civil War battles.
- More than doubled the membership in 3 years.
- Promoted to role of General Robert E. Lee in my third year (youngest ever).

Personal

- Jazz pianist (12 years of lessons); avid alpine skier.

APPENDIX E

Sample Addenda

GOOD ADDENDUM

Dear Sir or Madam:

I am writing to you to explain why my fall grades my junior year do not compare favorably to the rest of my transcript.

That semester, my younger sister collapsed one day in the grocery store with seizures and was rushed to the hospital. She was eventually diagnosed with a benign but large brain tumor, and for several months I flew home (more than two thousand miles away) once a week to be near her and help my parents and siblings through this ordeal. She has since been recovering and is regaining some of her mobility, and I am glad I was able to be there for her. However, my grades took a nosedive that semester, and in hindsight, I now realize that I should have taken the semester off rather than try to juggle all my responsibilities.

I wanted to let you know my family circumstances during that semester so that you have the full picture when evaluating my transcript. Please let me know if you have any questions.

BAD ADDENDUM

I understand that students must write these sorts of statements all the time, and I suppose after you read enough of
them, they must all sound like variations on the same
theme. Part of me realizes that there is little I can do or say
to erase the disastrous impression imparted by my LSAT Report, but I implore you to consider my circumstances.

Unfortunately, I was struck by an intestinal illness just
two days before the exam. I had no prior indication that I
was about to get sick and the illness was of such a severity
that had it not been for the test and the necessity of taking
it in order to get my applications in early, I might well have
been hospitalized. I now realize that entrance in the fall of
2001 was unrealistic; but I didn't see it that way then, and
because I wanted my application to be in reasonably early,
the October LSAT was my last opportunity. Because of the
side effects of the drugs I was taking, I knew during the
test that I was severely underperforming, but I decided not
to cancel the score because I was determined to apply this
fall.

I realize that this addendum must seem woefully inade-
quate, but I'm sure you agree that my score simply does not
capture my performance when I am at my best. In any event,
I believe the LSAT is less a predictor of my future success
than are my grades, especially in light of my senior thesis,
which only 15 percent of seniors at my school elect to do.

Index